CAPITALISM AND THE TRANSFORMATION OF AFRICA

TITLES IN THIS SERIES
Edited and introduced by Mary-Alice Waters

Capitalism and the Transformation of Africa

REPORTS FROM EQUATORIAL GUINEA

Mary-Alice Waters
Martín Koppel

PATHFINDER

NEW YORK   LONDON   MONTREAL   SYDNEY

ISBN 978-1-60488-016-8
Library of Congress Control Number 2008943729
Manufactured in the United States of America

First edition, 2009
Second printing, 2009

FRONT COVER: Evinayong, Equatorial Guinea, October 12, 2005:
Parade celebrating the country's independence from Spain in 1968.
In foreground, contingent of oil workers employed by ExxonMobil.
(Martín Koppel/*Militant*)

BACK COVER: Top to bottom, oil platform off coast of Equatorial
Guinea; participants at opening of First Equatorial Guinea Book
Fair, October 2005; graduation ceremony, National University of
Equatorial Guinea, August 2008; Guinean medical students and
Cuban internationalist health workers, August 2008; extensive
road construction cuts geographic isolation. (Credits: top and
bottom, *La Gaceta de Guinea Ecuatorial*; others, Martín Koppel/
Militant).

COVER DESIGN: Toni Gorton

Pathfinder
www.pathfinderpress.com
E-mail: pathfinder@pathfinderpress.com

CONTENTS

MARTÍN KOPPEL/MILITANT

MARTÍN KOPPEL/MILITANT

BRIAN TAYLOR/MILITANT

Mary-Alice Waters (*top left*) and Víctor Dreke (*top right*) giving presentations at 2005 Equatorial Guinea book fair. **BOTTOM**: Martín Koppel (*at left*) talking with 2008 graduate from National University of Equatorial Guinea.

ABOUT THE AUTHORS

Mary-Alice Waters is editor of the magazine *New International* and president of Pathfinder Press. A member of the Socialist Workers Party since 1964 and of the SWP National Committee since 1967, she has carried central responsibilities for the party's international work. Joining the Young Socialist Alliance in 1962, she was editor of the *Young Socialist* (1966–67) and served as YSA national secretary and then national chairperson (1967–68). From 1969 through the early 1970s Waters was editor of the *Militant* newsweekly.

Waters is the author, among other titles, of *Is Socialist Revolution in the U.S. Possible?*, *Pathfinder Was Born with the October Revolution*, *Che Guevara and the Imperialist Reality*, and *Feminism and the Marxist Movement*. She has edited and contributed to dozens of Pathfinder titles, including: *Rosa Luxemburg Speaks*; *Cuba and the Coming American Revolution*; *Cosmetics, Fashions, and the Exploitation of Women*; *The Changing Face of U.S. Politics*; *Capitalism's World Disorder*; and a series that has now grown to nineteen titles on the Cuban Revolution and its place in world politics.

Martín Koppel is managing editor of the *Militant* newsweekly and is a Spanish-language editor of both Pathfinder Press and of the magazine *Nueva Internacional*. He is a member of the National Committee of the Socialist Workers Party.

Of Argentine background, Koppel grew up in the United States. He joined the Socialist Workers Party in 1977. Before coming onto the *Militant* staff in 1991, he was a steelworker and member of the United Steelworkers of America. Koppel has traveled extensively in Latin America and the Caribbean covering political developments from Cuba to working-class actions in Puerto Rico, Argentina, Brazil, Paraguay, Mexico, the Dominican Republic, Nicaragua, and Grenada.

Koppel is the editor of *Puerto Rico: Independence Is a Necessity* by Rafael Cancel Miranda and *Habla Malcolm X*. He is the author of *Peru's Shining Path: Evolution of a Stalinist Sect*.

Víctor Dreke became involved as a teenager in the underground struggle and revolutionary war that overthrew the U.S.-backed Fulgencio Batista dictatorship in Cuba in 1959. In the early 1960s he commanded the volunteer units of workers, peasants, and youth that defeated the CIA-organized counterrevolutionary bands in the Escambray mountains of central Cuba.

His participation in Africa's freedom struggles began in 1965 as a leader of the column of Cuban internationalist volunteer combatants that fought in the Congo alongside the anti-imperialist supporters of slain Congolese leader Patrice Lumumba. Dreke was second in command of that column under Ernesto Che Guevara. In 1966–68 Dreke headed Cuba's military mission in Guinea-Bissau—then fighting for its independence from Portugal—and the Republic of Guinea (Guinea-Conakry).

Since 1990 he has served in various capacities as a representative of the Cuban Revolution throughout Africa. Dreke was Cuba's ambassador to Equatorial Guinea from

October 2003 until August 2008. He is vice president for international relations of the Association of Combatants of the Cuban Revolution and vice president of the Cuba-Africa Friendship Association.

INTRODUCTION

Capitalism and the Transformation of Africa: Reports from Equatorial Guinea is not an account of how centuries of colonial domination, the slave trade, and imperialist pillage have ravaged the peoples of Africa and plundered the natural resources of the continent. That history, in all its brutality and with all its consequences, has been lived by countless millions and documented thousands of times over.

The authors do not pretend to be experts on Equatorial Guinea, much less on the vast and richly diverse African continent.

We do not cast the toiling people of central Africa as helpless victims. Nor do we call on our readers to join the chorus of wealthy rock stars and imperialist-funded NGOs weeping over Africa's misery.

Our focus is quite different. We spotlight the transformation of the instruments of production and the new class relations emerging today in Equatorial Guinea. We look at the working class, drawn from the four corners of the earth, that is beginning to develop—in the same measure as a bourgeoisie is being formed, together with expanding layers of traders, middlemen, and professionals.

This is a book about the future being forged in the present. It is about the fight to make it a future that advances the interests of toiling humanity, different in all ways from the only past we have known. It is about the heightened expectations and the growing confidence, pride, consciousness, and combativity of the women and men who are themselves both agents and products of this ongoing transformation.

In 2005 and 2008, during two trips to Equatorial Guinea recorded in these pages, the authors and the reporting teams we were part of had the opportunity to see with our own eyes these accelerating changes, and to talk with hundreds of people whose lives are today deeply affected by them.

Equally important, those visits enabled us to see and record the living example of Cuba's socialist revolution, without which the road forward for working people in Africa, as elsewhere in the world, would be far more difficult to discern. The hand of proletarian solidarity extended by the more than 230 Cuban internationalists working in Equatorial Guinea as doctors, nurses, medical technicians, teachers, electricians, and others registers the kind of social relations—and human beings—that only a socialist revolution can produce.

When spun together, these seemingly disparate threads—the beginning transformation of production and class relations in Equatorial Guinea, and the practical example of Cuba's socialist revolution—produce the rich and complex fabric from which the future not only of Africa but the rest of the world will be cut.

~

Barely fifteen years ago, it was confirmed that vast deposits of oil and natural gas lay beneath the continental shelf surrounding Equatorial Guinea. U.S. oil companies contracted with the government to exploit those resources, making the country the third-largest oil producer in sub-

Saharan Africa today, trailing only Nigeria and Angola. In the blink of an eye, historically speaking, one of the most capital-intensive, technologically complex, and highly monopolized international industries has been superimposed on a foundation of labor productivity that was the product of thousands of years of hunting, fishing, and subsistence agriculture—and on largely precapitalist social relations distorted by centuries of colonial domination and inhuman trafficking by African and European slave traders to meet the labor demands of plantation owners in the Americas.

Royalties and other income from the exploitation of oil and natural gas are now being used in part by the government of Equatorial Guinea to begin to develop the basic infrastructure on which modern industry and rising labor productivity depend: electrification, paved roads, modern deepwater ports, cell-phone and high-speed communications networks, safe water distribution and sewage disposal systems, primary health care and improved medical facilities, the establishment of a national university, a medical school, public libraries. And more.

As this process advances, to put it in the words of the Communist Manifesto, "all fixed, fast-frozen relations, with their train of ancient and venerable prejudices and opinions, are swept away, all new-formed ones become antiquated before they can ossify."

The millennia-old social formations begin to dissolve as changing class relations emerge, full of glaring unevennesses, contradictions between old and new, and increasing class antagonisms.

What draws one's attention above all in Equatorial Guinea today is not the expanding exploitation of the country's natural resources, as striking as that is. Far more pervasive, and far more important historically, is the evidence that as the people of Equatorial Guinea are drawn inexorably into the world market—and as the legacy of colonial domination, which thwarted such a development for centuries, recedes—a modern capitalist class structure is emerging. More than 160 years ago, Karl Marx and Frederick Engels, the young founders of the modern working-class movement, who gave voice to its line of march, charted the birth of capitalism in Europe with unmatched insight and eloquence, as they lived through its heady expansion across the globe. Capital comes into the world, Marx wrote, "dripping from head to toe, from every pore, with blood and filth." The constant revolutionizing of the instruments of production that drives its never-ending search for profits is attained at the expense of the lives, limbs, and livelihoods of the class of propertyless laborers it creates.

Throughout each stage of class society, from slavery to feudalism to capitalism, Engels wrote, "every advance in production is at the same time a retrogression in the condition of the oppressed class, that is, of the great majority."

But Marx and Engels were the last to decry the tremendous advances in the productivity of social labor engendered by the rise of capitalism. To the contrary, they had nothing but contempt for those they dubbed "reactionary socialists" who wailed against the inhumanity of the factory system in order to sentimentalize the harsh, life-stifling, mind-deadening backwardness of precapitalist society. Globalization, far from an evil to be condemned and resisted, was recognized as the lifeblood of the international working class.

"The bourgeoisie has, through its exploitation of the world market, given a cosmopolitan character to production and consumption within every country," the Communist Manifesto proclaimed. "In place of the old wants, satisfied by the productions of the country, we find new wants, requiring for their satisfaction the products of distant lands and climes. In place of the old local and national seclusion and self-sufficiency, we have intercourse in every direction, universal interdependence of nations. And as in the material, so also in intellectual production. . . . National one-sidedness and narrow-mindedness become more and more impossible."

"The bourgeoisie, during its rule of scarce one hundred years," the Manifesto continued, "has created more massive and more colossal productive forces than have all preceding generations together. Subjection of nature's forces to man, machinery, application of chemistry to industry and agriculture, steam navigation, railways, electric telegraphs, clearing of whole continents for cultivation, canalization of rivers, whole populations conjured out of the ground—what earlier century had even a presentiment that such productive forces slumbered in the lap of social labor?"

To see even elements of such a transformation unfolding in parts of Africa today, "dripping from every pore with blood and filth," is not cause for hand-wringing despair. It is further evidence of the growing size and strength of the working class internationally. "In proportion as the bourgeoisie, i.e., capital, is developed, in the same proportion is the proletariat, the modern working class, developed—a class of laborers who live only so long as they find work and who find work only so long as their labor increases capital."

And wherever on earth this process unfolds, the Manifesto says, this "organization of the proletarians into a class" also gives rise over time to the independent social and political organization of a proletariat that has started to become conscious of itself—to the "self-conscious, independent movement of the immense majority, in the interests of the immense majority."

Today the working class in more and more parts of Africa is expanding, as is the migration of working people from one country to another within Africa, as well as to Africa from Asia, the Middle East, and beyond. At the same time, growing numbers of African immigrants are strengthening the working classes of more and more imperialist countries.

The intertwining of all these experiences is of even greater importance today as the most devastating global contraction of capitalist production in some three-quarters of a century accelerates worldwide. The toll already being felt by toilers in the imperialist countries will be worse for those of the semicolonial world, and more destructive than during the last great world capitalist depression of the 1920s and 1930s. Eighty years ago the large majority of the people of Africa, still dominated by European colonial masters, lived on the margins of the world market, at best, where the vicissitudes of capitalist production touched them less directly. Today, as the soaring cost of food and plunging raw materials prices attest—to take but the most obvious examples—that is no longer the case.

Decades of wars, economic, social, and political crises, explosive class battles, and revolutionary struggles lie ahead of us. The international strength, self-consciousness, and political independence of the working class—and the clarity, discipline, and courage of its vanguard—will be decisive to the outcome. As the beginning transformation of Equatorial Guinea helps underscore, the toilers of Africa will have greater weight in shaping that future than ever before.

∾

Class society "has never been anything but the development of the small minority at the expense of the exploited and oppressed great majority; and it is so today more than ever before," Engels explained in *The Origin of the Family, Private Property, and the State.* That has been true since the days, shrouded in the unrecorded mists of prehistory, when cattle and women first became the private property of a few men. Today, when it is factories employing thousands, vast tracts of farmland in the tens or hundreds of thousands of acres, and mines producing millions of tons of coal, metals, and other raw materials indispensable to modern industry that are the private property of capitalist families the world over, Engels's observation seems even more obvious.

The revolutionary conquest of political power by the workers and farmers of Cuba on January 1, 1959, marked one of the greatest leaps in history toward putting an end to those millennia of successive class societies. Over the next two years Cuba's working people and their government expropriated the vast majority of the plantations, factories, mines, public transport, banks, and utilities held as private property by the capitalist families of the United States and Cuba. They successfully defended their course against the military assaults and economic warfare organized by the most brutal imperial power on earth. It was these decisive actions first by hundreds, then thousands and millions, that made possible the steps they have taken over the last five decades to begin constructing a society built on a different class foundation. A society driven not by the dog-eat-dog, blind laws of capital, but one based on the conscious social solidarity of the toilers.

That class solidarity—to cite but one example especially pertinent to the account in this book—is what defines the character of the primary care and medical education that some 38,000 doctors, nurses, dentists, and lab technicians trained by the Cuban Revolution are bringing to the most remote and inaccessible regions of some seventy-three countries around the world, Equatorial Guinea among them.

How has Cuba—with its limited economic resources, and in face of unceasing aggression by Washington—been able to create a medical system acknowledged around the world for its excellence? How has it been able to train doctors and nurses who are not only willing but eager to travel to the most isolated regions of the world to provide medical services? Why is no other country on the face of the earth capable of anything similar?

The answer was explained with unmatched clarity by Ernesto Che Guevara, the great Argentine-Cuban revolutionary leader who fought at the side of Fidel and Raúl Castro in the revolutionary war and early years of the new government. "To be a revolutionary doctor, . . . there must first be a revolution," Che told an audience largely composed of Cuban medical students and health workers in 1960. And make a revolution is exactly what Cuban working people did. Their economic, social, and political accomplishments since then—from health care and education, to aid given freedom fighters the world over—have been possible only because they took the power to rule out of the hands of the landlords and capitalists.

One of the great ironies of history may well be a coincidence no one could have predicted. The most far-reaching revolutionary victory in the Americas—alive and advancing despite all odds—celebrates its fiftieth anniversary just as the leaders of the Yankee empire that set out to destroy it are plunged into the worst economic and social crisis they have faced since the one that culminated in World War II.

∿

The reporting team to Equatorial Guinea in 2005 included Jonathan Silberman, director of Pathfinder Books in London, and *Militant* reporters Brian Taylor and Arrin Hawkins, in addition to Martín Koppel and myself. In 2008 the other members were *Militant* reporters Omari Musa and Brian Taylor. The articles, notes, and photographs brought together in these pages were a collective effort—produced amid fast-moving events and under the press of weekly, or often daily, deadlines. The end product is enriched by the efforts, observations, and insights of all.

In late 2005 and early 2006, members of the first reporting team also went on the road to share their experiences in Equatorial Guinea with some 500 people at five large regional meetings that took place in Atlanta, San Francisco, Minneapolis-St. Paul, New York, London, Edinburgh, and Stockholm. These were followed by a number of smaller meetings on university campuses across the United States, many sponsored by African and African-American student groups, as well as invitations to speak to college and high school classes in the United Kingdom and Sweden.

These experiences helped underscore for all of us the interest in and thirst for knowledge about the struggles and advances of the peoples of Africa today among significant layers of workers and youth in the imperialist countries.

∾

We would like to express our special appreciation to the dozens of Equatorial Guineans who spent many hours helping us to better understand a country and society that was new to us all. Too numerous to name in their entirety, the patient aid and generous hospitality they offered made our trips possible, productive, and enormously enjoyable.

First and foremost our thanks go to President Teodoro Obiang Nguema, who made time to receive us and respond to numerous questions about the government's development plans. His answers and explanations, which enriched our understanding, are woven throughout the articles included here.

Minister of Information, Culture, and Tourism Jerónimo Osa Osa Ekoro went out of his way to arrange not only the interview with President Obiang, but our visits to important areas of the country such as the new international airport at Mongomeyen and the site on the Wele River where the hydroelectric dam will be built.

Rector Carlos Nse Nsuga and Vice Rectors Trinidad Morgades and Pedro Ndong Asumu, along with the entire staff of the National University of Equatorial Guinea, welcomed us on both visits and invited us to participate together with them in many activities.

Poet and essayist Carmela Oyono Ayíngono and historian Rosendo-Ela Nsue Mibui generously offered their time and historical insight.

Cuba's Ambassador to Equatorial Guinea Víctor Dreke, First Secretary Ana Morales, members of the embassy staff, and numerous Cuban internationalist volunteers living and working in Equatorial Guinea shared their knowledge, their solidarity, and many hours of work and travel with us on both occasions.

Whatever limitations, errors, or misunderstandings the book may contain, we hope our friends and colleagues in Equatorial Guinea will laugh at our ignorance and help us correct them. Our sole intention has been to produce a book that—in the United States and other imperialist countries especially—can bring to life for working people and youth repelled by the daily brutalities and indignities of capitalism an understanding of the elements of the present and future we glimpsed in Equatorial Guinea.

Mary-Alice Waters
January 2009

PHOTOS: DAVE WULP/MILITANT

After visiting Equatorial Guinea in 2005, members of the reporting team spoke at regional meetings in Atlanta, San Francisco, Minneapolis-St. Paul, New York, London, Edinburgh, and Stockholm about their experiences on the trip. The events were attended by some 500 people.

PHOTOS: Meeting at Spelman College in Atlanta, Georgia, November 2005. **TOP:** Chairperson James Harris at podium. At speakers table, left to right, reporting team members Arrin Hawkins, Mary-Alice Waters, Brian Taylor, and Martín Koppel. **BOTTOM:** Sarah Thompson, president of Student Government Association at Spelman, joins discussion from the audience of nearly 100.

PART I

Background

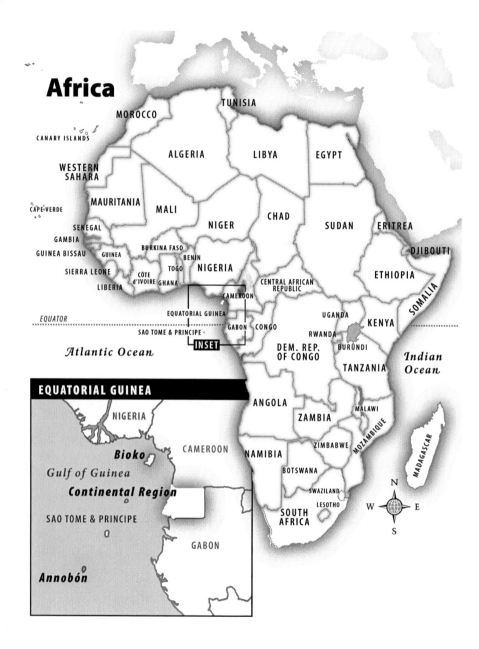

Africa

TUNISIA
MOROCCO
CANARY ISLANDS
WESTERN SAHARA
ALGERIA
LIBYA
EGYPT

CAPE VERDE
MAURITANIA
MALI
NIGER
CHAD
SUDAN
ERITREA

SENEGAL
GAMBIA
GUINEA BISSAU
GUINEA
BURKINA FASO
BENIN
NIGERIA
DJIBOUTI

SIERRA LEONE
CÔTE d'IVOIRE
TOGO
GHANA
CENTRAL AFRICAN REPUBLIC
ETHIOPIA

LIBERIA
CAMEROON

EQUATORIAL GUINEA
UGANDA
KENYA
SOMALIA

EQUATOR
SAO TOME & PRINCIPE
GABON
CONGO
RWANDA
BURUNDI

INSET
DEM. REP. OF CONGO
TANZANIA

Atlantic Ocean
Indian Ocean

ANGOLA
ZAMBIA
MALAWI
MOZAMBIQUE
MADAGASCAR

ZIMBABWE
NAMIBIA
BOTSWANA
SWAZILAND
LESOTHO
SOUTH AFRICA

EQUATORIAL GUINEA

NIGERIA
Bioko
CAMEROON

Gulf of Guinea
Continental Region

SAO TOME & PRINCIPE
GABON

Annobón

N
W E
S

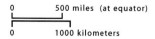

0   500 miles (at equator)

0   1000 kilometers

Background on Equatorial Guinea

BATA—Equatorial Guinea has a population of around one million. Both geographically and numerically, it is one of the smallest countries in Africa today. It is made up of the Continental Region (formerly called Río Muni), the island of Bioko—where the capital Malabo is located—and several other smaller islands in the Gulf of Guinea. Tribal, clan, and language ties ignore the borders this former Spanish colony shares with the neighboring countries of Cameroon and Gabon, formerly colonized by France.

The languages of daily life for the big majority are Fang (86 percent), Bubi (6.5 percent), and other indigenous languages.

Two major dialects of Fang are spoken in the country. On Bioko many speak Bubi, while pidgin English is spoken there by a minority, the Fernandinos, descended from slaves and contract laborers brought to the island by the British from the region that today is Sierra Leone. Ndowe (3.6 percent) and other languages are spoken along the continental coast. The inhabitants of Annobón island (1.6 percent) speak Annobonese, partially derived from Portuguese.

A majority of Guineans in urban areas also speak Spanish, which is the language of schooling. Some speak French as well. Spanish and French are the two official languages for state business and legal purposes.

The island of Bioko (long called Fernando Poo after its Portuguese "discoverer") was a staging post for the world trade in chattel slaves from the seventeenth to the early nineteenth century. The ports of what is now Equatorial Guinea came under Portuguese, Spanish, British, and Dutch colonial rule at different times. When the European powers partitioned Africa among themselves at the Berlin Conference in 1885, this region—designated Spanish Guinea—became the only part of the continent south of the Sahara "owned" by Spain.

The Bubis and Fang put up strong resistance to the European slave traders and to the claims of the colonizers. It was only in 1926 that Madrid took full control of the continental territory.

From 1939 to 1968 Spanish Guinea was under the dictatorship of the clerical-fascist Francisco Franco, whose regime in Spain lasted until his death in 1975. The Spanish colonizers kept the area isolated from the world and brought little market activity beyond Spanish-dominated logging and the cultivation of cacao and coffee, virtually all for export. Guineans were denied elementary rights. Most were designated the legal equivalent of minors— wards of the colonial state—with no right to acquire or sell property, enter into contracts, or control their own wages. They were subject to forced labor.

Equatorial Guinea gained independence from Spain in 1968. The first Guinean government, headed by President

October 12, 1968, ceremony in Bata marking Equatorial Guinea's independence from Spain and the end of almost 500 years of colonial domination by Portuguese, Dutch, British, and Spanish rulers.

Francisco Macías Nguema, became an eleven-year reign of terror. Declaring himself president for life and even referring to himself as a "socialist" on occasion, Macías cloaked his Pol Pot–like repression in anti-Spanish, anticlerical, and anti-"white" demagogy. Churches and schools were closed, and any Guinean—especially any non-Fang—with even a few years of education became a special target of repression. Many were jailed, tortured, or executed. Tens of thousands of Guineans fled into exile. In a country that, after centuries of colonial and imperialist domination, was already one of the most ravaged in Africa, even minimal trade and agricultural production for the market collapsed.

"Under the dictatorship, many had lost hope and even thought the colonial past had been better," President Teodoro Obiang Nguema noted in an August 5, 2008, speech here in Bata.

On August 3, 1979, Macías was overthrown in a coup by young Guinean officers led by Obiang. Most Equatorial Guineans mark that date as the beginning of the work to initiate modern development of the country.

Equatorial Guinea

Bioko

Punta Europa

MALABO ✪

Rebola

Baney

Pico Basilé
3,011 m ▲

Luba

Riaba

Caldera
2,261 m ▲

Moka

0	5		10 miles

| 0 | 5 | 10 | 15 | 20 km |

Continental Region

Río Campo

CAMEROON

Gulf of Guinea

Micomeseng

Ebebiyin

Nsoc Nsomo

Nkimi

BATA ✪

Niefang

Añisok
Mongomeyen

Atlantic

Ocean

Mbini

GABON

Wele River

Monte Alen ▲

Mongomo

Evinayong

Akonibe

Nsork

Kogo

Akurenam

GABON

San Antonio
de Palé

Annobón

0	10	20	30 miles

| 0 | 10 | 20 | 30 | 40 | 50 km |

0	2 km

| 0 | 1 mi |

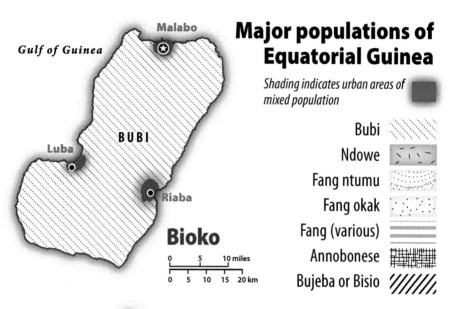

**Major populations of
Equatorial Guinea**

*Shading indicates urban areas of
mixed population*

Bubi	
Ndowe	
Fang ntumu	
Fang okak	
Fang (various)	
Annobonese	
Bujeba or Bisio	

Gulf of Guinea

Malabo

Luba

BUBI

Ríaba

Bioko

0   5   10 miles
0 5 10 15 20 km

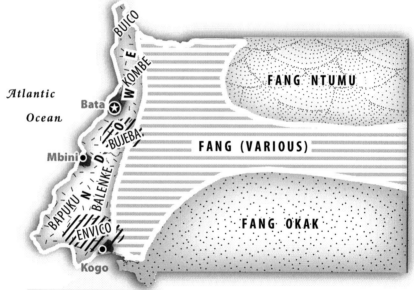

Atlantic
Ocean

BUICO

W KOMBE

Bata

BUJEBA

Mbini

NDOWE

BAPUKU

BALENKE

ENVICO

Kogo

FANG NTUMU

FANG (VARIOUS)

FANG OKAK

Continental Region

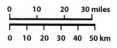

0   10   20   30 miles
0 10 20 30 40 50 km

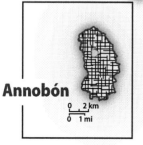

Annobón

0   2 km
0   1 mi

PART II

Transformation of production and class relations

In the 1990s vast offshore oil and natural gas reserves were discovered in Equatorial Guinea's waters. U.S. oil companies contracted with the government to exploit these resources, bringing rapid and substantial change to economic infrastructure and class relations. Oil doesn't have to be "a curse," said President Teodoro Obiang Nguema. It can be "a blessing" if used to develop infrastructure and lay the foundation to expand agriculture and industry.

TOP: Port facilities to serve West and Central Africa oil industry being built in deep-water bay at Luba, 2005. **BOTTOM LEFT:** Paved roads being extended throughout Equatorial Guinea, including regions never before accessible by car or truck. **BOTTOM RIGHT:** President Obiang during August 7, 2008, interview with authors.

Transformation of production and class relations highlights realities facing millions in Africa

by Martín Koppel

BATA, Equatorial Guinea—"Some in the international press say that oil is a curse" for a country like Equatorial Guinea, said the president of this Central African country, Teodoro Obiang Nguema. "The curse would be the misuse of that resource." If used to develop the country's economic infrastructure and lay the foundation for the expansion of agriculture and industry, he noted, it can be "a blessing."

Obiang was responding to a question posed by Mary-Alice Waters, president of Pathfinder Press, during an August 7, 2008, interview that was part of a two-week fact-finding trip across Equatorial Guinea.

Supporters of the New York–based publisher had returned to this country to follow up on an initial visit three years ago to take part in the country's first-ever book fair, held in October 2005 at the National University of Equato-

Published in the Militant, *September 8, 2008.*

rial Guinea in the capital city of Malabo. They welcomed the opportunity to learn more about the rapid economic and social changes under way in this nation long ravaged by the world's dominant capitalist powers, and to help widen knowledge among working people in the United States and other imperialist countries of the struggle being waged today by the peoples of Africa.

Legacy of superexploitation

Equatorial Guinea, a former colony of Spain, is one of the smallest countries in Africa, both geographically and in population. Until a decade and a half ago, it was also what President Obiang called "the poorest of the poor"— one of the least economically developed regions on this continent. There were few paved roads, electrification was largely a dream, there was virtually no industry—even light manufacturing—and land cultivation was subsistence agriculture. There was no modern bourgeois class structure—no rising class of risk-taking merchants, factory owners, and landowners, no wageworkers or peasantry. The legacy of centuries of colonial and imperialist domination maximized the hobbling and great unevenness of the country's social relations and economic structure.

Then, in the mid-1990s, vast reserves of oil and natural gas were discovered deep beneath the country's offshore waters in the Gulf of Guinea. This increased the ability to substantially expand production and trade, and at the same time deepened economic and social contradictions.

Flying into Malabo international airport today, you glimpse the oil platforms of ExxonMobil and other companies dotting the sea. Marathon's liquid natural gas plant lights the sky at nearby Punta Europa, center of the U.S. oil companies' operations in Equatorial Guinea.

Within a few years' time, one of the world's most capital-intensive, technologically complex, and highly monopolized industries has been superimposed on a foundation in which the existing productivity of labor is a product of millennia of hunting, fishing, and subsistence agriculture, distorted by centuries of slave trading and colonial domination.

At night the blazing lights of Punta Europa are visible across the bay to tens of thousands of Malabo residents who still lack drinkable running water, modern sanitation, paved streets, or more than sporadically reliable electricity.

Returning to Equatorial Guinea after several years, we noted four striking developments above all: the changing class relations and composition of the working class here, with workers drawn from around the world; the resources going into development of the economic infrastructure; the expansion of the system of higher education; and the spread of these developments throughout all parts of the country.

These changes and the contradictions they engender—revolutionizing conditions of life for many—underscore realities facing millions in large parts of Africa today.

They also help explain why Equatorial Guinea faces no dearth of enemies. The country most recently hit world headlines when British mercenary Simon Mann was sentenced here to thirty-four years in prison for his admitted role in organizing a failed coup, one in which Mark Thatcher, son of former British prime minister Margaret Thatcher, is also implicated. The plotters, armed and funded by overseas interests seeking to control and profit from exploitation of Equatorial Guinea's oil, aimed to install as government figurehead Severo Moto, a Guinean bourgeois oppositionist now living in Spain.

Speaking to the press on the eve of Mann's trial, Obiang said he "strongly suspected" that government agencies in

Britain, Spain, and the United States were fully aware of the coup being planned and did nothing to stop it or to warn the government of Equatorial Guinea.

Changing class structure

Equatorial Guinea remains a country with virtually no manufacturing. There is a brewery, a water bottling plant, and a cement factory crippled by shortages of imported primary goods. Furniture-making shops and sawmilling operations that produce lumber for construction remain small-scale handicraft operations. With land cultivation beyond subsistence farming largely nonexistent and more than half the population now living in urban centers, almost all food is imported from Cameroon, Spain, and elsewhere. Transportation costs magnify the impact of rising world food prices. The chicken we ate one day came from Brazil. Eggs were from Cameroon.

Those living in rural areas, largely still outside the market, get food from hunting small forest animals or fishing, and from plantains, cassava, malanga, and other plants that grow easily on small pieces of cleared land at the forest's edge. Most of these foodstuffs are directly consumed, not bought or sold. Along rural roads and in sprawling town markets, many people sell small quantities of remaining food products as well as other goods to scrape by.

At the same time, in less than fifteen years the exploitation of oil and natural gas reserves has turned Equatorial Guinea into the third-largest oil exporter in sub-Saharan Africa, after Nigeria and Angola. "It is U.S. companies that are operating the offshore extraction operations, including ExxonMobil, Marathon, and Hess," Obiang noted in the interview. Marathon also owns the liquid natural gas and methanol plants. In recent years, he added, "a number of other companies have signed agreements with [state-owned] Gepetrol, including Malaysian, South African, and Nigerian oil companies," for joint exploration and development projects. China is the largest purchaser of the country's oil.

Exploitation of Equatorial Guinea's oil resources has accelerated the development of a modern class structure here in the urban areas. While tribal and clan ties continue to dominate social relations in the countryside, these preclass formations dissolve more and more with the increased penetration of the world market and capitalist relations of production.

As has happened in other parts of the world over the past five centuries, capital accumulation is today consolidating a capitalist class in Equatorial Guinea, with expanding private holdings in land, hotels, construction, transport, and other businesses. Through the purchase and exploitation of labor power, this rising class is extracting surplus value and expanding its wealth.

There are growing numbers of small traders, merchants, lawyers, and other petty-bourgeois layers. Drawn by the oil boom, this includes increasing numbers from West Africa, the Middle East, China, and other parts of the world.

A class of wageworkers is being born in Equatorial Guinea, too. As the Communist Manifesto noted about Europe and North America more than 150 years ago, "In proportion as the bourgeoisie, i.e., capital, is developed, in the same proportion is the proletariat, the modern working class, developed—a class of laborers, who live only so long as they find work and who find work only so long as their labor increases capital."[1]

Capitalist expansion inexorably draws growing parts

1. Karl Marx and Frederick Engels, *The Communist Manifesto* (New York: Pathfinder, 2008), page 39.

of the world into its orbit, Karl Marx and Frederick Engels noted. Today capital is exerting its pull on Equatorial Guinea. Increasing numbers of Guineans are becoming wageworkers for the first time ever, as laborers on road and other construction projects especially. Nearly half the country's population lives in Bata and Malabo, which are being swelled by stepped-up migration from the countryside of toilers seeking jobs.

The demand for labor has also led to a large influx of workers from abroad, especially from other parts of Central and West Africa—including Cameroon, Gabon, Burkina Faso, Mali, and Nigeria. Workers from Paraguay, the Dominican Republic, and elsewhere in Latin America have come to work in hotels, restaurants, and at other jobs. On all the construction sites we visited, most of the skilled workers and technicians are migrants from French-speaking African countries or contract employees from China, North Africa, Lebanon, Iran, and elsewhere.

As Obiang said in an August 5, 2008, speech to an audience that included many Guinean construction workers, "Equatorial Guinea used to be a country that was held in contempt." Now, he said, "many are coming here in search of prosperity. We have more immigrants than other countries in Africa. It's like bees who are coming to taste our honey."

The growth of the working class and its increasingly international character—as workers bring their skills and experiences from other parts of the world—has increased the pride and confidence of working people here. It is widening their scope.

What a road system opens up

During our trip we heard many Equatorial Guineans, from students to government officials, express their concern that the resources from the oil bonanza that began more than a decade ago be used to lay the foundations for expanded production that can sustain the people of Equatorial Guinea in the future, whatever the ups—and downs—of the world market. The goal of investments in the country's basic infrastructure is to benefit ordinary Guineans, Obiang noted, and to foster the development of capitalist corporate enterprises. "We want small Guinean companies to become large ones," he said.

In the more than ten cities, towns, and rural areas we visited across Equatorial Guinea—from Bata and Malabo, the largest cities, to Ebebiyin, Mongomo, Evinayong, Añisok, Niefang, Mbini, and Kogo on the continent, as well as Luba on the island of Bioko—there was evidence that substantial resources are going into building or upgrading roads, electric service, cellular phone transmission towers, hospitals, modern deepwater port facilities, airports, and schools. These and other projects are having an impact on the quality of life of an increasing number of Guineans. Their expectations are being raised.

The most visible change from three years ago is the extensive building and paving of roads. Major stretches connecting the main cities and towns, many miles of which were previously rough tracts of dirt rendered impassable in rainy months, have now been paved. Many more miles, often through difficult mountainous terrain, are under various stages of construction. Most of that work has been contracted out to capitalist enterprises from Egypt, France, China, and other countries.

For hundreds of thousands, especially in the rural areas, the upgrading of the road system means increased mobility and easier access to health-care centers, schools, markets, and jobs.

"It used to take a whole day to travel the 200 kilometers

[125 miles] from my hometown to Bata," said Antonio Nsue Nsue Ada, editor of the university publication *Horizontes*, who is from Ebebiyin in the northeast. "Now it takes three hours."

We traveled to the southwestern town of Kogo to visit a hospital where a Cuban volunteer medical brigade is working. Just a few years ago, according to Cuban doctors who accompanied us, visitors had to travel there by water, usually by canoe. Our thirty-mile trip by van along the coast from Mbini, on what had previously been little more than a footpath, took more than two hours on a washboard dirt road currently under construction. And the trip will become shorter once the road is paved.

In colonial times, the remote island of Annobón was the place where slaves too old or sick to work were sent to die; later it became a place of forced exile for independence fighters. Until recently, travel to Annobón was infrequent, unsafe, and time-consuming. "The only transportation was a ship that went every three months," Obiang noted. "Now there is an airstrip on Annobón, with two flights a week."

Airports in Malabo and Bata are also being upgraded, and a new international airport, with a runway capable of landing the largest passenger and freight planes, is under construction in Mongomeyen near the eastern city of Mongomo. In addition, the deepwater ports of Bata, Malabo, and Luba are being expanded to facilitate further growth of the oil industry and develop international trade between Equatorial Guinea and the broader region. "The port of Malabo," Obiang said, "will be the largest and deepest port in western Africa."

Electrification: a major challenge

In most of sub-Saharan Africa, less than 5 percent of the rural population has access to electricity, and Equatorial

Guinea is no exception.

"Electrification is an elementary precondition if modern industry and cultural life are to develop," notes Jack Barnes in "Our Politics Start with the World," the lead article in issue 13 of *New International* magazine. Electrification means being "able to decide whether to stop a meeting because it's getting dark. To have the possibility to study and work comfortably after sundown. For children to do their schoolwork or to read to each other in the evening. Simply to pump water to village after village, saving countless hours of back-breaking work for every family, and especially for women and girls."

In Equatorial Guinea, the reality of this challenge and its importance becomes apparent when driving through the countryside at night, even along the main roads. In each cluster of homes many are dark, while in others a single light is shining or a kerosene lamp casts a shadow in a room.

There is no nationwide electric service; each city and town relies on its own generators. In most towns, electricity is available only five hours a day, from 6:00 p.m. to 11:00 p.m., and even then many homes are not connected to any power source.

Local residents gave us one example after another of what this means for everyday life. Many students cannot do their homework at night, or must travel to some other home or center where light is available. Food cannot be refrigerated. Surgery and many other medical procedures cannot be performed in hospitals during the day, unless they have a functioning diesel generator for emergency situations, which many don't. Computers, where they are available, cannot be used in daylight hours, and for only a few hours in the evening.

In the town of Añisok in the north-central region, Dr.

MARTIN KOPPEL/MILITANT

BRIAN TAYLOR/MILITANT

TOP: Djibloho, site on the Wele River where hydroelectric dam is under construction to provide energy for all of continental Equatorial Guinea and neighboring areas of Cameroon and Gabon. Reporter Omari Musa is at left.

BOTTOM: With little but subsistence agriculture in the country, virtually all food sold on the market is imported, including at roadside stalls such as these in Bata.

Amarilis Contreras, a Cuban physician who staffs the medical center there, told us that "when there is no power, we use kerosene lamps or flashlights to do our work. We sterilize our instruments with boiling water." Even the provincial capitals of Mongomo, Ebebiyin, and Evinayong have power for just twelve hours a day, from about 6:00 p.m. to 6:00 a.m. Malabo and Bata now have electrical generators operating twenty-four hours a day, but they are hit by frequent blackouts because of generating power and distribution networks inadequate to meet growing demand. We directly experienced all these facts more than once.

Along rural roads, women can frequently be seen walking long distances with enormous baskets of firewood on their backs to provide fuel for cooking and other household needs—another reminder of how vital electrification and increased productivity of labor are to the emancipation of women, as well.

One of the highest-priority development projects under way is a hydroelectric dam at Djibloho, near the district capital of Añisok. Harnessing the power of the Wele River, it is expected to provide electricity for all of continental Equatorial Guinea as well as areas of Cameroon and Gabon. It will be the single biggest step so far toward establishing a nationwide electrical grid.

Pedro Mba Obiang Abang, the national assembly delegate for Añisok district, drove us to the site where the dam and hydroelectric plant are due to be completed in four or five years. The lead contractor, he said, is a Chinese enterprise.

"The Chinese government has lent us $2 billion to finance the development of the electrical system, including the hydroelectric plant," President Obiang informed us.

A recently arrived twenty-six-member Cuban volunteer

brigade of electrical technicians is working with the state-run electrical company, SEGESA. In a July 31 meeting in Bata with several brigade members, José Luis García Chaviano, who heads the group working on the continent, told us that their job was to train Guinean technicians in upgrading the electrical infrastructure and administering the distribution system. As in many countries where working people lack electricity, there is no centralized control over its distribution, and jerry-rigged extensions and hook-ups run everywhere, with the safety problems, fire hazards, and accidental deaths by electrocution such practices entail.

"The system of underground electrical cables here in Bata is high-quality, but the foreign companies that built it went away without leaving the plans and diagrams. Nor did they provide training in maintenance or safety," said Ricardo García, one of the Cuban electricians. "We are training technicians in maintenance, without which the equipment will be damaged more and more."

"Our priority is people's safety and health," insisted Wilfredo Arbelo. "We train everyone in safe methods, from the managers to the workers, including the most basic steps such as wearing helmets and gloves."

Expansion of university system

Expansion of the National University of Equatorial Guinea (UNGE) is another notable change of the last three years. The university was founded in 1995, soon after the discovery of oil.

"You cannot have development without skilled cadres," Obiang said. "That is why we had to create the national university." Noting that many at the time thought it was an adventure for Equatorial Guinea to establish its own university, he continued, "We now have 3,000 trained graduates."

On August 5, 2008, another 102 students graduated from the National University, receiving degrees in agronomy, teaching, humanities, engineering, environmental sciences, medicine, and other fields. María Jesús Nkara, director of academic affairs, reported that the university now has 2,275 students—double the number from three years ago. To increase the capacity, two new campus facilities are being built, one in Malabo and another in Bata. Nkara drew attention to the fact that 42 percent of the university students are women. To applause from the audience, she added that it is gratifying that a small but growing number of graduates from the school of technical engineering are female and now work for the electric company, "doing the same work as the men, including climbing ladders and electric poles."

Addressing the graduating class, President Obiang noted that when Equatorial Guinea gained independence forty years ago, there were fewer than a dozen university graduates in the country. Trinidad Morgades, today UNGE vice rector of the Malabo campus, was the only one with a university degree in humanities at the time. Those seeking university education had to go to Spain or elsewhere abroad to study, and few returned to Equatorial Guinea.

Knowledge of that history, and of what their graduating class represented for the future of their country, filled the students and faculty with evident pride.

"We had to work very hard at the medical school," said Tecla Mangue Mitogo, 26, as she waited for the graduation ceremony to begin. "We had to learn to study."

"Now I'm glad I will be contributing to my country as a doctor," she said. "I'm waiting to find out what city I will be asked to work in."

Students graduating as teachers, engineers, agronomists,

and in other fields expressed similar pride in what their training meant.

"Of the twenty students who began together in the oil engineering course, only four of us are graduating today," Marcos Esono Ndong told us. "Seven or eight dropped out after the first year, and another six or so the second. The course was too hard, and overcoming all the material obstacles was too much. Several others learned enough of the basics to get hired by one of the big international oil companies and left. Four of us finished and will work for the development of our country."

Young Guinean doctors are key to building a public health system

by Martín Koppel and Mary-Alice Waters

BATA, Equatorial Guinea—"This is the first time we've had doctors working in this city," said Antonio Oyono Esono, a Guinean health ministry official, speaking to a group of visitors at the public hospital in Ebebiyin, a district capital in the northeast corner of this Central African country.

Oyono was pointing out that the public health system in Equatorial Guinea is being built through the growing numbers of Guinean doctors, graduates of the new medical school here, who today are working with volunteer Cuban medical personnel in cities and towns across the country.

We had the opportunity to visit hospitals and clinics and talk with doctors, nurses, and medical technicians working in nine different regions of the country, in the process learning about the expansion of public health programs here.

Published in the Militant, *September 22, 2008.*

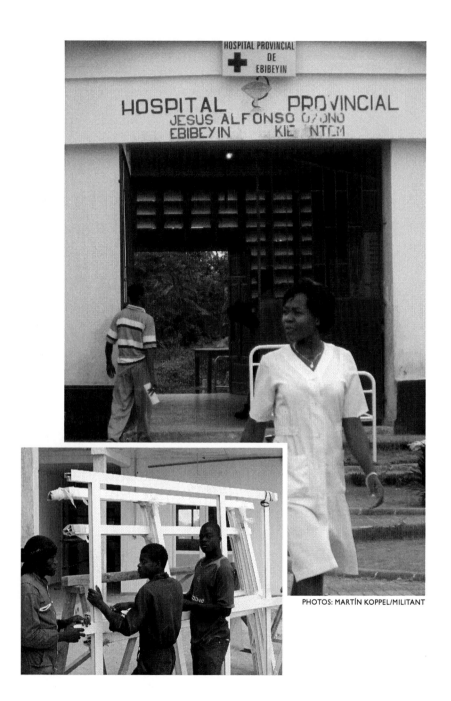

PHOTOS: MARTÍN KOPPEL/MILITANT

Numerous hospitals across Equatorial Guinea are undergoing major rebuilding and expansion. **TOP:** Jesús Alfonso Oyono Hospital in Ebebiyin. **BOTTOM:** Workers rebuilding hospital in Evinayong.

Imperialism's toll in Africa

Equatorial Guinea shares with the rest of Africa a centuries-long legacy of colonial and imperialist domination. The health conditions facing the peoples of the continent today are a graphic expression of this history. Every year millions in sub-Saharan Africa are killed by preventable or curable diseases. More than 3 million people die yearly from HIV/AIDS, tuberculosis, or malaria, according to the World Health Organization (WHO). The AIDS pandemic has particularly ravaged southern Africa. In Zimbabwe, for example, an estimated 20 percent of women between the ages of 15 and 49 are infected with HIV, and about the same percentage in South Africa.

Diarrheal diseases—preventable with clean water and simple hygienic measures—are another leading cause of death, especially among infants. More than 40 percent of the population of sub-Saharan Africa lack access to safe water, according to WHO estimates, and the reality is undoubtedly worse. Widespread malnutrition contributes to the ravages of disease at all ages.

Of the twenty countries with the highest maternal mortality rates in the world, nineteen are in Africa. Some 43 percent of the world's children who die before reaching the age of five are African. Infant mortality rates are as high as 165 per 1,000 live births in Sierra Leone and 154 in Angola, compared to the national average of 6.9 in the United States. Life expectancy at birth, which stands at 79 in the United Kingdom, is reported to be 45 in Nigeria and 38 in Angola.

Equatorial Guinea, while far from the worst-off on the continent, lives with this same legacy. Until a decade and a half ago, paved roads and telephone service barely existed, let alone access to health care. Few outside the two largest cities had access to electricity.

During the first years following independence from Spain in 1968, several hospitals were built in the largest provincial towns by the government of Francisco Macías Nguema. But what became an eleven-year reign of terror under Macías led to the deterioration of hospitals and clinics and the exodus of trained medical personnel. No institutions of higher learning had ever existed in the country, and few Guineans who managed to study abroad, whether in medicine or any other field, returned to the country.

Malaria endemic in region

As in much of Central Africa today, malaria is endemic in Equatorial Guinea. Typhoid fever, tuberculosis, and intestinal parasites are also widespread. HIV/AIDS, though less severe than in many other countries of sub-Saharan Africa, is increasing. Only 28 percent of the population has access to sanitation services, and even in urban areas water available through municipal distribution systems is not safely drinkable. It must first be boiled or chemically treated. According to *La Gaceta de Guinea Ecuatorial*, a magazine widely circulated in this country, average life expectancy at birth is 54 years.

Since the discovery in the mid-1990s of substantial oil deposits beneath the continental shelf and territorial waters surrounding Equatorial Guinea, the government has used considerable resources, largely derived from revenues from petroleum production, to develop the country's infrastructure. Upgrading the health-care system has been one of the goals.

A broad program of medical cooperation between the governments of Equatorial Guinea and Cuba was established in 2000. Cuba agreed, among other things, to send medical brigades to help staff hospitals and public health centers throughout Equatorial Guinea. Today 160 Cuban doctors, nurses, and lab technicians are working in all eighteen of the country's districts, including the most remote areas. The brigades, which are as large as seven or as small as two—a doctor and a nurse—live in the communities they work in, sharing the conditions of life of the population.

The cooperation agreement also included establishment of a medical school here in Bata, the largest city, as a professional school that is part of the national university. Its purpose is to train hundreds of Guinean doctors and nurses to progressively replace the Cuban medical personnel who provide almost all primary medical care.

Guinean doctors today lead hospitals

Since August 2006, when the first class of seventy-three students graduated from the medical school, dozens of Guinean doctors have begun working at health-care centers across the country side by side with the Cuban physicians, nurses, and technicians. Their combined efforts are already having a palpable impact.

The medical director of every public hospital we visited was a recently graduated Guinean doctor, and we were told this is true in other districts as well. Their confidence was striking, and their solid medical training is beginning to transform relations within communities in ways they described with optimism.

In Evinayong, a provincial capital of 36,000 inhabitants in the south-central region, the medical director of the hospital is Dr. Santiago Nguema Ndong, a native of that city. We had met him on a previous visit in October 2005, as he and nineteen classmates were about to leave for Cuba for their final year of medical school.

"Malaria is the number one health problem we face," Nguema told us. "It is the main cause of infant mortality."

In areas where the medical brigades have been working for the last eight years, Nguema and others reported, the number of infant deaths has begun to be reduced, due to the timely treatment of more patients and through preventive efforts. Statistics on such questions, however, are often unreliable throughout much of sub-Saharan Africa. This is another of the challenges now being taken on by district hospital staffs as they keep records and begin to compile more accurate figures.

World Health Organization statistics for 2006—the most recent available—give the overall infant mortality rate for Equatorial Guinea as 123 per 1,000 live births. Records compiled by the medical brigades, however, show that in 2002 the average for infants cared for by the hospitals and clinics serviced by the brigades was 47 per 1,000 live births. By 2007 that figure had been reduced to 16.5 per 1,000. In the territory served by the Evinayong medical brigade, infant mortality was 35 per 1,000 for the first half of this year.

María Elena Núñez, a nurse working in Evinayong, reported there had been only one maternal death at that hospital in the past year and a half. This is a significant achievement in a country where, according to WHO estimates, the number of maternal deaths is 880 per 100,000 live births.

Impact of lack of electricity

The prevalence of many diseases long ago eradicated in the advanced capitalist countries is primarily due to the absence of any infrastructure providing safe drinking water, sewage disposal, or the systematic eradication of disease-carrying insects. The lack of electrical power, reliable means of communication, and passable roads compounds the difficulties.

Outside the two major cities of Malabo and Bata, electricity is available in most towns a few hours a day. In the largest provincial capitals—Ebebiyin, Mongomo, and Evinayong—generators, when running, provide electricity for twelve hours a day, from 6:00 p.m. to 6:00 a.m. Elsewhere it is usually available, at best, five hours a day, from about 6:00 p.m. to 11:00 p.m. As the medical personnel in Ebebiyin pointed out to us, that means doctors cannot perform even emergency surgery during the day, unless the hospital has a functioning diesel generator, which many don't.

"When you have to draw blood from a patient at night to run a lab test, it's hard even to find the vein when you have only a flashlight or a kerosene lamp," Dr. Amarilis Contreras told us during our visit to the north-central town of Añisok.

At the hospital in Niefang, doctors showed us a brand-new incubator for premature infants that had been donated some time ago by ExxonMobil, one of the major U.S. companies exploiting deepwater petroleum deposits in Equatorial Guinea. The machine was sitting in the hallway, still tightly wrapped in protective plastic. Without reliable, round-the-clock electricity, it was unusable, the head of the pediatric unit explained. And ExxonMobil donated neither a generator nor the fuel to keep one running.

As noted in the previous article, there is no national electric system in Equatorial Guinea; each city and town relies on its own generators. A hydroelectric project, currently being built near Añisok, is expected to provide electricity for continental Equatorial Guinea when it is completed some five years from now.

In Kogo, in the extreme southwest corner of the country, the terrain and transportation difficulties make it hard for patients from the surrounding area to get to the hospital. Kogo is an isolated town on the edge of a river delta with extensive mangrove swamps. Sleeping sickness, which is transmitted by tsetse flies, and mosquito-borne malaria are even more prevalent than in other parts of the country. Cuban doctors, who have been trained to work and provide care under even the most difficult conditions, travel by canoe to hard-to-reach villages. (Some 1,500 volunteered to do so in 2005 in Mississippi and Louisiana following Hurricane Katrina—an offer impudently rejected by Washington).

"We often made trips that took four hours by boat, then a long walk," Dr. William Pérez, a Cuban volunteer who worked in Kogo, told us. "I had the bitter experience of seeing a child who died on the way to the hospital because the trip took six hours."

Now, for the first time, the narrow coastal path between Mbini and Kogo is being turned into a paved road that will be passable year round.

In several towns we were told by medical personnel that many patients who test HIV-positive cannot afford to go to Bata, the only city on the continent where a reliable diagnosis can be made and appropriate treatment initiated.

Expanding medical knowledge

Doctors in every town we visited explained that one of the challenges they face is convincing local residents to come to the hospital or clinics for medical treatment. Many, they said, have grown up accepting disease and death at an early age as a fact of life. Superstition and confidence in traditional tribal healers, known as *curanderos*, lead many patients to come for medical help only when it is already too late. That is a major reason many children die of malaria, which is usually not fatal if treated in time.

"Last July a 27-year-old teacher here died from AIDS," Dr. Contreras told us in Añisok. "She had gone to a curan-

TOP: Graduation ceremony in Bata for 102 members of the class of 2008 of the National University of Equatorial Guinea. At left, graduating medical school student Tecla Mangue receives diploma from university rector Carlos Nse Nsuga. Aim of the medical school is to train hundreds of Guinean doctors and nurses to replace Cuban personnel currently providing almost all primary health care.

BOTTOM: Guinean medical students, 2005, preparing to leave for Cuba for their final year of medical studies. In striped shirt, Leonardo Ramírez, head of Cuba's medical collaboration in Equatorial Guinea at that time. Second from right, Ana Morales, first secretary of the Cuban Embassy, who is herself a doctor.

dero instead of the hospital. We often hear people call AIDS 'the bad luck disease.'"

Systematic popular awareness efforts have helped convince greater numbers of people to go to the hospitals and clinics for treatment. Dr. Juan Álvarez Morell, head of the medical brigade in Evinayong, said brigade members speak on "weekly radio programs and give talks at the hospital and in the community to educate about infant malaria, diarrhea, and other health problems. We promote our vaccination campaigns."

A notable change is happening as young Guinean doctors take charge of hospitals and integrate themselves in medical programs around the country. They are reaching out to traditional curanderos and *parteras* (midwives) to win their confidence and train them to recognize medical conditions that need immediate hospital care. The young doctors are working to convince traditional healers to help get people to go to the hospital and clinics. Results vary from area to area. But Dr. Marcelino Edjang Ondó, the hospital director in Niefang, reported they have had success there in working with the curanderos.

"Traditions don't change overnight," said Dr. Dayamí Escalona, head of the medical brigade in Niefang. "We find ways to link our use of modern science and the work of the curanderos to win their cooperation."

That the Guinean doctors most often grew up in the area, speak the indigenous language as their mother tongue, and are known in the community is a great aid in gaining the confidence of patients and the cooperation of traditional tribal leaders in working with the curanderos and parteras.

Rebuilding hospitals

Major rebuilding and repair work was under way in about half the hospitals we visited. In three towns—Mongomo, Evinayong, and Luba—the old structures had been gutted, and largely new buildings were going up inside the shell. The dilapidated condition of almost all public hospitals in the past is slowly being transformed—a measure of the resources the government of Equatorial Guinea is putting into upgrading the primary health-care system.

The gap between facilities available to working people and to those with substantial wealth, Guineans and foreigners alike, was brought home to us, however, by a visit to the Centro Médico La Paz. This ultramodern private hospital here in Bata, an Israeli-run project organized in collaboration with the government of Equatorial Guinea, opened at the end of 2007. A similar hospital is under construction in Malabo.

Most of the thirty-five doctors on the hospital staff—in their majority Israeli, with some from Argentina, Uruguay, and other countries—are not resident in Equatorial Guinea. They fly into Bata for a few days or weeks at a time. Three of the doctors are Guineans, recent graduates of the medical school here.

We toured the Centro Médico La Paz following the signing of a research agreement between the hospital and the national university. Noting that they had performed neurosurgery there just the day before, director Alon Stamler told us that the hospital is equipped to do the most advanced procedures, making it possible for patients seeking the best-quality care to stay in the country instead of going abroad. Stamler remarked that the international oil companies, whose personnel work sometimes dangerous jobs on offshore platforms, would be among the most appreciative of the medical services the center offers, adding that the new hospital in Malabo hopes to establish long-term corporate contracts with these firms.

The hospital is pay-as-you-go. One night's stay costs

$325, an X-ray $200, a doctor's visit $225, a CAT scan $350. Many Guineans live on less than a dollar or two a day. Few beds were occupied in the wards we were shown.

In a conversation after the guided tour, two professors from the national university who had taken part in the visit told us they were proud this facility now made such advanced care available in their country. When asked who would be able to afford it, however, they ruefully replied, "Hardly anyone."

Need to train specialists

In the district public hospitals, the number of operations being performed has doubled over the past eight years. But Dr. Juan Carlos Méndez, head of the Cuban medical brigade in Equatorial Guinea, noted that most of these are minor procedures. For serious operations, patients still must go to Bata, where the hospital has surgeons and more advanced equipment.

"We need to train more surgeons and other specialists for our hospitals," said Dr. Edjang of the hospital in Niefang, where three doctors, two Cuban and one Guinean, are working.

Building on the initial progress, this challenge is being addressed at the medical school in Bata, where several students have now finished their first year of training in surgery, internal medicine, or obstetrics/gynecology.

Cuban medical cooperation: the internationalist example of a socialist revolution

by Martín Koppel and Mary-Alice Waters

BATA, Equatorial Guinea—"It took a lot of effort and will-power. We had to learn how to study, and how to study long hours. But today we're graduating as doctors. We will be working to improve the health of the Guinean people," said Benjamín Ntutumu Mbá.

His remark captured the pride and confidence of the 21 doctors who graduated August 5 from the medical school here. They were among 102 students in the class of 2008 at the National University of Equatorial Guinea (UNGE) who received their diplomas. Now they are starting their first jobs as MDs at hospitals and clinics across the country.

The university's medical school in Bata, led and staffed by Cuban doctors for almost a decade, opened in 2000 as part of a program of medical cooperation between the governments of Equatorial Guinea and Cuba. Cuba com-

Published in the Militant, *September 29, 2008.*

MARTÍN KOPPEL/MILITANT

JUVENTUD REBELDE

Nearly 160 Cuban doctors, nurses, and laboratory technicians, part of medical cooperation program between governments of Equatorial Guinea and Cuba, provide services throughout the country, including rural areas and small towns where such care has previously been inaccessible and unaffordable.

TOP: Guinean medical students Fulgencio Nsue Mba and Armando Nsue Ela *(third and fourth from left)* together with Cuban medical brigade at hospital in Ebebiyin, 2008. Also standing at back are Tebelio Concepción, dean of medical school *(left)* and Ademar Agüero *(center)*, head of Cuban medical brigades in Continental Region.

More than 38,000 Cuban medical personnel are working in 73 countries around the world, including 1,500 in 35 African countries. **BOTTOM:** Cuban doctors in Guatemala in 1999, in aftermath of Hurricane Mitch.

mitted itself to send brigades of doctors, nurses, and lab technicians—today they number 160—to help staff hospitals and public health centers throughout this Central African country. The medical school is training hundreds of Guinean doctors and nurses whose goal is to progressively replace the Cuban personnel currently providing almost all primary health care.

The training of Guinean doctors, committed to improve health conditions in their country, is no small achievement in one of the least industrialized countries in sub-Saharan Africa. Equatorial Guinea shares with the rest of the region a centuries-long legacy of colonial and imperialist domination. As in much of Central Africa, malaria is endemic, typhoid fever, tuberculosis, intestinal parasites, and sleeping sickness are widespread, and the incidence of HIV/AIDS infection, while lower than in much of the region, has been increasing.

The health-care crisis inherited by Guineans is magnified by the very workings of the world capitalist system. Drawn by the lure of much higher salaries, better living conditions, and enticements of personal "career" advancement, medical personnel migrate to imperialist countries from Africa and other parts of the semicolonial world. The head of Ghana's public health service, for example, reported in 2005 that the country had lost 30 percent of doctors trained there to the United States, Britain, Canada, and Australia. Some 5,300 physicians from sub-Saharan Africa were practicing in the United States alone, according to a 2004 study by Human Resources for Health.

The training offered by the Cuban-run medical program, like the Cuban Revolution itself, imbues students with a different class perspective. Instead of promoting personal "advancement," it is based on social solidarity and providing health care as a human right. It seeks to instill a determination to bring medical services to working people in isolated rural areas and small towns for whom such care has previously been inaccessible and unaffordable. The medical school program is organized in close cooperation with the Ernesto Che Guevara medical school in Pinar del Río, Cuba. When the program was first launched, a group of Guinean students studied five years in Pinar del Río and their sixth under supervision of the medical school faculty in Bata. Simultaneously another group studied five years in Equatorial Guinea and spent their final year in Pinar del Río.

Today all students attend the school here and then complete their sixth year in Cuba, reported Dr. Tebelio Concepción, dean of the program in Bata. Concepción, a Cuban dentist who previously taught at the Ernesto Che Guevara school, noted that since the founding of the institution in Bata, its dean has always come from Pinar del Río as part of that university's long-term commitment to the program of cooperation.

In the 2007-2008 term, 170 Guinean students were enrolled in the Bata medical school, including 23 in a five-year nursing program. More than half the students—89—were women, a statistic greeted with enthusiasm and pride at the Bata graduation ceremony when announced by María Jesús Nkara, UNGE director of academic affairs. For the 2008-2009 academic year, the student body has grown to 202, with the largest first-year class since the medical school was established.

With the August 5 graduation, 122 Guinean medical students have received their diplomas here since 2006.

High retention rate
"The big majority of all the medical students complete the course," Concepción told us. This contrasts with many

other university departments in Equatorial Guinea, where, for a variety of reasons, a large percentage of students drop out in the first or second year.

At the heart of this success, Concepción said, is the individualized attention given to each student as they transform their study and work habits. The Cuban instructors provide tutoring to all students who need assistance. To make this help more effective, "the professors, grouped according to each year of study, meet monthly to discuss how their students are doing and to determine who needs special attention," he said. The students select a representative to take part in these discussions and help uncover problems needing attention that the teachers may not be aware of.

A student, for example, may be living in a neighborhood without electric service and cannot study at home in the evenings. "Or sometimes a student whose first language is Fang has a more limited knowledge of Spanish, and has a hard time understanding a Cuban professor who talks very fast." Fang, with two major dialects, is the main indigenous language spoken in the region of the African continent that includes Equatorial Guinea.

"This kind of individualized attention has been decisive in giving us a high retention rate," noted Dr. Juan Carlos Méndez, head of the Cuban medical brigade here, who previously directed the ministry of public health in the Cuban province of Ciego de Ávila.

Graduates of the medical school we talked with said the help and encouragement they received from their teachers had been decisive in their ability to overcome myriad obstacles and complete their studies. Such obstacles are often outside the experience, assumptions, and consciousness of even sympathetic observers from countries dominated by class relations shaped by capitalist production and trade.

Equatorial Guinea does not have a class of small landowning agricultural producers struggling to grow a surplus to sell on the market in order to pay off debts and not lose their land. An industrial working class is only now barely beginning to emerge. These historical realities mean that the habits of work imposed on the toilers by the capitalist whip of debt slavery for the peasantry, and job competition and wage slavery for the working class, exist only in embryo in large parts of Central Africa.

Dr. Florentino Abaga Ondó, a Guinean who is today medical director of the hospital in Mbini, a coastal town on the continent, is one of the 2006 graduating class who studied five years in Cuba and returned here for the sixth. What he found most difficult when he began his studies in Cuba, he told us, was not the food or cultural differences, or being far from family and friends. It was "learning to work, learning to work hard. That's what real study is." He also felt the pressure of being one of the few African students in his class at the Latin American Medical School,[2] he said—feeling he had to prove he wouldn't wash out as some of his fellow students expected. He succeeded, and attributed this in large part to the backing and encouragement of his teachers.

"The most difficult thing in my first year was to adjust to the method of study," said Tecla Mangue Mitogo, who graduated August 5. "We had to get used to reading and studying at least five hours a day.

---

2. The Latin American Medical School was established by the Cuban government in 1999 to train doctors, free of charge, from Latin America and elsewhere in the world. Currently it has students from over two dozen countries. The sole requirement is for students to agree to put their training to use in poor and working-class communities of their countries of origin. The enrollment is close to 10,000 students, with 1,500 graduating each year.

"The Cuban professors helped us a lot. They taught us to study and to work."

Extension program

Today dozens of Guinean physicians are working at health-care centers across the country, alongside Cuban doctors, nurses, and technicians. At every public hospital we visited, the medical director, often still in his twenties, was a Bata medical school graduate. That is now true throughout the country, we were told.

Starting this year, another important step is being taken. A full medical school program is being offered in five more cities for young people who would not have been able to overcome barriers preventing them from living and studying in Bata, whether financial and housing limitations, family responsibilities, or whatever.

Dr. Méndez reported that 13 students are enrolled in the program so far: 2 in Ebebiyin, 3 in Mongomo, 1 in Mbini, 5 in Malabo, and 2 in Luba. Next year the program is projected to expand to additional towns, with an increased number of students in each.

On a visit to several towns in the Continental Region, we met several of these students and their instructors. We accompanied the rector of the National University of Equatorial Guinea, Carlos Nse Nsuga, and a group of professors and administrators on a tour of the university extension centers in Ebebiyin, Mongomo, and Mbini. The university personnel were assessing the first months of the new program.

The medical courses are taught by Cuban doctors working in those districts. Many have extensive teaching experience in Cuba as well as years of medical practice. In Kogo, for example, the nurse recently arrived from Cuba, with more than thirty years of experience, had previously been head of nursing administration for all of Havana. In Mongomo three students are enrolled in the extension program, which began in May with a three-month preparatory course. Dr. Luisa Gómez, one of the Cuban doctors leading the program there, told us the preliminary studies include chemistry, biology, an introduction to medicine, and computer training. Beginning their practical education right from the start, the students accompany the doctors each morning as they make their rounds and treat patients at the hospital clinic. Classes are held in the afternoon, after the doctor-instructors finish their hospital consultations for the day.

José Fernando Monsuy, twenty-four, a student in Mongomo, said he had already learned a lot from going into the community with Cuban doctors to educate local residents on basic hygiene and preventive health care.

University rector Nse Nsuga urged the students to speak not only about the progress they are making but the problems they confront. "If you don't raise them, we can't together address them," he said.

The students described various practical obstacles. Their new classroom is still under construction, as part of the hospital's renovation. In the meantime, two computers, which they use to watch instructional DVDs, are temporarily set up at the modest residence of the Cuban medical personnel. They can use these computers only after 6:00 p.m., when electricity comes on for the evening.

Students pointed to other problems, as well. There is a lack of textbooks. The room serving as a school library is often locked during hours they are able to use it. After some discussion, the rector encouraged the students to take some control in busting through these impediments. He urged them to make a proposal on library hours and then arrange with hospital administrators to assign someone to have a library key. He suggested they organize themselves to photocopy and share reading materials. The medical director, Dr. Nicéforo Edjang, a Guinean graduate of the school in Bata, also responded to the three students. There is a basis to your complaints, he said. But the heart of what underlies them is that you are unaccustomed to the discipline of study, which takes work.

"You have to adjust to what it means to study," Edjang said. "That's your biggest difficulty. All of us who went to the medical school faced the challenges you are going through. In fact, the conditions we confronted in the first year were even harder," Edjang said. For example, that very first class, we learned on a previous visit to Equatorial Guinea in 2005, had no textbooks at all for the initial six months.

The students agreed to take the suggestions of the rector and initiate solutions to the obstacles they were raising.

Medical personnel in several cities we visited pointed out that training students in their home towns, as opposed to a distant city, let alone another country, strengthens their commitment to work in their own communities. Educating doctors ready to work in areas most in need of healthcare facilities is a cornerstone of the medical training they receive.

In Kogo, for example, the small hospital now has one Guinean doctor who is also the director—an important gain. He grew up in a different region, however.

"We need to train more doctors who are from here and who will stay here," Dr. Hilario Nguema told us. It makes a big difference to have doctors who grew up in the community and are known. In the Kogo area it helps to have personnel who speak Ndowe, the first language for many in the coastal region.

Méndez said students training in their home towns

"know their own communities and are committed to them. Seeing what others like them have been able to achieve will speed the process of winning more medical students to the program and training even more doctors. And it will strengthen the public health system, especially in areas that have had little access to trained medical personnel."

'We'll stay as long as needed'

At the end of our two-week tour, Méndez and Concepción took time from their busy work schedules with the medical brigades posted throughout the country and at the school in Bata to tell us a little more about the work Cuban volunteers are carrying out.

The medical cooperation between the Cuban and Guinean governments, they emphasized, aims to train Equatorial Guinean doctors and nurses who will work to transform public health care in their country. This is a principle guiding all Cuba's medical missions in every country where they are invited to work, they noted.

To accomplish this goal, Méndez said, "we are committed to stay as long as necessary."

Such medical collaboration is an expression of the proletarian internationalist course that has marked Cuba's socialist revolution for half a century.

In 1963 the very first Cuban medical brigade volunteered to go to Africa. They went to newly independent Algeria, less than a year after the French colonial regime had been defeated by the Algerian National Liberation Front in a long and bitter war.

That same year, Cuba responded to a request by Algeria's workers and peasants government to send weapons and volunteer combatants to help deter an imperialist-backed assault by the Moroccan regime. Over the decades, Cuban internationalists have fought alongside anti-imperialist forces throughout Africa—from the Congo to Guinea-Bissau to Angola—as well as in Latin America.[3] That tens of thousands of Cuban medical personnel are today providing health care in the most hard-to-reach parts of countries the world over is one of the most demonstrative expressions of the socialist character of the revolution that Cuban workers and farmers carried out, overturning capitalist property relations and transforming the consciousness of millions. No other country in the world is capable of anything remotely comparable, nor does any other government want to do so.

As Cuban revolutionary leader Ernesto Che Guevara, himself a physician, explained and demonstrated by his own example, "To be a revolutionary doctor, you must first make a revolution."[4] In Cuba not only has health care—an expensive commodity under capitalism—become free

---

3. Beginning in the mid-1960s, Cuban volunteer combatants served in a number of African countries to support national liberation struggles for independence and sovereignty. These included the Congo, Guinea-Bissau, and Ethiopia. The largest such effort was in Angola, where, between 1975 and 1991, some 375,000 Cuban volunteer combatants helped defend that country against repeated South African invasions and an insurgency backed by Washington and other imperialist powers.

In the decade following the victory of the Cuban Revolution in 1959, Cuban internationalist volunteers also fought alongside revolutionary forces in Latin America, including in the Dominican Republic, Argentina, Bolivia, and Venezuela.

4. See *Che Guevara Talks to Young People* (Pathfinder, 2000). A Rebel Army commander in Cuba's revolutionary war to overthrow the U.S.-backed Batista tyranny, after the 1959 triumph, Guevara held major responsibilities in the new government. In 1965 he led the Cuban column fighting alongside anti-imperialist forces in the Congo. In 1966–67 he headed a detachment of internationalist combatants in Bolivia. Wounded and captured by the Bolivian army during a CIA-organized operation on October 8, 1967, he was murdered the following day.

and available to all as a basic right, but those who become medical workers are educated in that spirit.

As of 2008, more than 38,000 Cuban doctors, dentists, nurses, and medical technicians are working as volunteers in 73 countries, according to Cuba's Ministry of Health. That includes 1,500 medical personnel in 35 African countries. Cuban personnel are responsible for medical schools not only in Equatorial Guinea but in Gambia, Guinea-Bissau, and Eritrea.

The Cuban medical brigade has been in Equatorial Guinea since 2000, Méndez told us, as part of the Comprehensive Health Program for Central America, the Caribbean, Africa, and Asia. That initiative had been launched by the Cuban government two years earlier in response to the destruction caused by Hurricane Mitch in Central America. "We sent emergency medical brigades to the region struck by the hurricane," he said, and from there the program expanded to other parts of the world.

Today the 160 doctors, nurses, and lab technicians who make up the Cuban brigade in Equatorial Guinea are working in all 18 of the country's districts—57 of them on the island of Bioko and 103 on the continent. Except for those with special leadership responsibilities, who sometimes serve longer, brigade members generally work here for two years, with a one-month vacation at the end of the first year.

"The Cuban doctors go to every corner of the country, even to the most remote areas," President Teodoro Obiang Nguema told us in an August 7 interview. "You can see the discipline and morale of those doctors."

The living expenses of the Cuban medical workers are paid by the government of Equatorial Guinea. "We provide them with a stipend, housing, transportation, and other necessities," Obiang said.

In addition to the minimal stipend—the same for all personnel, irrespective of qualifications—the Cuban government pays the Cuban medical volunteers their regular monthly salaries in Cuban pesos, giving that amount directly to their families in Cuba or depositing it in a bank account held for them until their return. Medical workers who have completed international missions receive 50 dollars a month in hard currency in addition to their salary in Cuban pesos.

Conquests of Cuban Revolution
In a discussion with more than thirty Cuban medical brigade members in Bata one evening, several talked about the deep impact the experience of working in Equatorial Guinea has had on them.

Some had previously served in Angola, Iraq, Western Sahara, Ethiopia, or other countries—one was on her fourth internationalist assignment. For most of them, however, it was their first time living and working outside Cuba. While they vary widely in age and work experience, most are in their forties or early fifties.

"Here we discovered a reality we ourselves had never encountered in Cuba," said Dr. Laura Cobo. "We've seen preventable diseases we had previously only read about in books. We've seen children dying of malaria or dying of hunger." Some of the doctors noted that many diseases common in Equatorial Guinea had ravaged working people in Cuba as well, before the socialist revolution triumphed in the early 1960s and began transforming social relations. Even the oldest of the brigade members, however, are generally too young to have experienced those capitalist conditions firsthand.

In Equatorial Guinea, Cobo said, Cuban medical personnel often treat patients for polio. "In our country it's been years since we've seen a case of polio. In Cuba children receive thirteen vaccinations in their first year."

One of the hardest experiences here, several doctors told us, was seeing children with malaria or other curable illnesses who were brought to the hospital too late to be successfully treated and died.

At the same time, Dr. William Pérez added, "there are cases of children in critical condition who, despite our limited resources, we are able to restore to health. That gives us tremendous satisfaction."

Dr. Rubén Romero told us he has been teaching in Bata two years. "This medical school is a big step forward. Now the third class of students is graduating," he said. "We can begin to see the fruits of our labor."

Cobo said the hardest thing she's had to get used to is that "health care here is a commodity." In Cuba high-quality medical care is free for everyone. But here "patients have to pay for everything, from medicine to emergency operations. If they can't pay we're not supposed to treat them."

Some doctors told us they find this so difficult to carry out that they not infrequently forget to tell patients they have to pay.

"This experience prepares us to work better on behalf of the Cuban Revolution," Cobo said. "When we return home, we'll be able to use these experiences—despite all the material shortages we face in Cuba—to explain the gains of the revolution," to explain what a socialist revolution means.

The conditions the Cuban doctors describe are the reality millions confront in Africa and other parts of the semicolonial world. Most satisfying of all, they say, is the opportunity to be part of changing this reality.

PART III

Without culture you cannot be free

A hunger for books, and aspirations of youth to understand the world and their place in it, marked the First Equatorial Guinea Book Fair in October 2005.

TOP: Part of audience at opening session of fair. **BOTTOM:** Pathfinder literature table, being staffed, left to right, by Brian Taylor, Arrin Hawkins, and Jonathan Silberman.

'To read is to grow'
is book fair banner

by Martín Koppel

MALABO, Equatorial Guinea—Several hundred students, teachers, and others took part in the First Equatorial Guinea Book Fair, October 17–20, 2005. The event was hosted by the university at its campus here in the capital of Malabo.

The four-day cultural event was organized to encourage reading and to promote literature and writers from Equatorial Guinea in particular. It featured book presentations, seminars, poetry readings, art displays, book sales, and ended with a skit written and performed by students.

Along the university's outdoor hallways were tables with books on Equatorial Guinean culture and history, as well as titles produced by Cuban publishers, books from New York–based Pathfinder Press, literature from the Catholic publishing house Ediciones San Pablo, works of art, and other materials.

The literary festival was timed to coincide with the an-

Published in the Militant, *November 7, 2005.*

niversary of Equatorial Guinea's national independence. Several days of celebration culminated October 12 in a massive and spirited march, an expression of national pride, held in the town of Evinayong, a provincial capital in the Continental Region of the country.

Some of the professors and other participants expressed surprise—and delight—in witnessing the thirst among young people for books on culture and politics in Equatorial Guinea and the world. A number said they hoped the fair would lead to establishing the country's first bookstore, and that future such events would have even more books by Guinean authors.

'Foster culture of reading'

The book fair, held under the banner "To read is to grow," was opened by the rector of the National University of Equatorial Guinea, Carlos Nse Nsuga. This was the first time such an event was being held in the country, he emphasized.

Also on the platform were Joaquín Mbana, the vice minister of education; Trinidad Morgades and Pedro Ndong Asumu, vice rectors of the university campuses in Malabo and Bata, respectively; Cuban ambassador Víctor Dreke; and Hwangbo Ung Bom, ambassador of the Democratic People's Republic of Korea. The audience included students from both the university and secondary schools.

The fair aims to promote reading, said poet Carmela Oyono Ayíngono in her introductory remarks. Reading and access to books are "indispensable for cultural development," she said. Every Guinean household needs a small library "to foster the culture of reading from an early age."

Two books presented the opening day helped set the tone of the entire event: *Historia de Guinea Ecuatorial: Período pre-colonial* (The history of Equatorial Guinea:

Precolonial period) by Rosendo-Ela Nsue Mibui, and *From the Escambray to the Congo: In the Whirlwind of the Cuban Revolution* by Víctor Dreke. The Cuban embassy in Equatorial Guinea was one of the sponsors of the event, which also coincided with Cuban Culture Day on October 20.

The opening day program also included a well-received presentation by Pathfinder president Mary-Alice Waters introducing Pathfinder Press to participants at the fair. On behalf of the five-person team taking part in the fair and staffing the Pathfinder stand, Waters said, "Our presence here helps underline that there are ordinary people in the United States who do not start from a desire to protect the relative wealth and abundance of resources consumed in the most economically developed countries.

"There are many, like ourselves, who understand that American and European development exists in substantial part because billions the world over live in crushing poverty," Waters said. "We start with the world and how to transform the international economic order, which is the source of this reality." (See page 83 for the text of Waters's remarks.)

Rosendo-Ela Baby spoke about *Historia de Guinea Ecuatorial*, written by his father, a well-known historian and a veteran of the struggle for independence from Spain. "This book explains events that led to the formation of our country," he said. It presents a wealth of facts on the period of preclass society—including the migration to Central Africa by the Fang, Bubi, and other Bantu-speaking peoples—that preceded the imposition of European colonial rule and the slave trade in what is now Equatorial Guinea.

Dreke presented *From the Escambray to the Congo*, an account of his five-decade-long record as a revolutionary fighter, published by Pathfinder Press. Visibly enjoying the opportunity to interact with a responsive audience of Guinean youth, Dreke outlined some of these experiences, from his involvement as a teenager in the revolutionary war that overthrew the U.S.-backed Batista dictatorship in Cuba in 1959, to his role as the commander of the volunteer units of workers and farmers that defeated CIA-organized counterrevolutionary bands in the Escambray mountains of central Cuba in the early 1960s.

"In 1965 the revolution and Fidel [Castro] gave me the tremendous opportunity of coming to Africa—to Congo-Léopoldville, today the Democratic Republic of Congo—to fight together with Commander Ernesto Che Guevara and a group of 130 Cuban compañeros under the leadership of the Congolese liberation movement," said Dreke, who was second in command of that column of Cuban internationalist volunteer combatants.[1] Most of the professors and many students in the audience knew of Dreke as the Cuban ambassador to their country, but knew nothing about his participation in African liberation struggles.

He pointed out that Cuba not only has some 140 internationalist volunteers—mostly medical personnel—serving in Equatorial Guinea today, but that "our goal is that our doctors, agricultural technicians, and others be re-

---

1. From April to November 1965, a contingent of Cuban volunteers under the command of Guevara went to the Congo to fight alongside and help train supporters of martyred prime minister Patrice Lumumba, who had been ousted and murdered over four years earlier in a coup supported and organized by Brussels and Washington. In 1965 these forces were battling U.S.-backed Belgian and South African mercenary armies that were trying to prevent the vast mineral wealth of the Congo from escaping imperialist control. Dreke's account of this mission is contained in the concluding chapter of *From the Escambray to the Congo*.

placed by Equatorial Guinean compañeros." Some seventy Guinean youth are currently completing their sixth year of medical studies in Cuba and in the Cuban-led medical school in Bata.

Dreke said the Cubans working in Africa today are not there to extract the region's oil wealth. "From Africa we have taken back to Cuba only two things: our dead—the more than 2,000 Cubans who have perished in combat in different African countries—and the hearts of the majority of Africans," he said to applause. (See page 91 for the text of Dreke's remarks.)

Wide-ranging discussions

Throughout the four-day event, the book presentations and seminars sparked lively discussions.

Rosalía Andeme, a professor at the university and part of the book fair organizing committee, spoke on "Folklore as an instrument of education and culture." She explained the origins of some of the Guinean dances and music in the resistance to the slave traders and colonial oppression.

Youth in Equatorial Guinea need to embrace their cultural heritage rather than be ashamed of it, Andeme argued. "Modernization does not have to mean Americanization or Europeanization of our culture."

Joaquín Mbana, the vice minister of education and one of the authors, presented the book *De boca en boca* (By word of mouth), a collection of essays and a contribution to Fang oral history. With a great deal of humor, appreciated by the students in the audience, Mbana explained that while the traditions recorded in its pages are part of the country's cultural heritage, beliefs in sorcery and magic are not unique to Equatorial Guinea—they exist in Europe and elsewhere—and can be given a historical explanation.

A panel of five professors discussed *Macías: verdugo o víctima* (Macías: executioner or victim) by Agustín Nze Nfumu, currently the Equatorial Guinean ambassador in London. The book, published last year, is about a subject until now rarely discussed in public here—the 1968–79 reign of terror under President Francisco Macías Nguema, head of the first government following independence from Spain.

During the Macías years, tens of thousands fled into exile and many, including those distrusted as "intellectuals," were jailed, tortured, or executed. Macías, whose government developed close relations with Moscow and Beijing, cloaked himself in anti-Spanish and anti-imperialist rhetoric. He made himself president for life and at one point declared himself a "socialist." On August 3, 1979, he was overthrown in a coup by young Guinean military officers and later tried and executed. The coup was led by Teodoro Obiang Nguema, today the country's president.

Another panel discussed *Mi vida por mi pueblo* (My life for my people), an autobiographical book by President Obiang.

In the discussions following these and other presentations, students asked probing questions of the panelists. Was Macías really a victim of his own personality, as the book suggests? What did they think about the state of democratic and union rights in Equatorial Guinea today?

In tribute to Cuban Culture Day, several presentations focused on Cuban history and culture, including the historical ties between the two former colonies of Spain.

A talk on "Black women as depicted in literature and art in nineteenth century Cuba," by Jassellys Morales, third secretary at the Cuban embassy, was one of the liveliest. She focused on slavery, sexual relations, marriage, and the racial intermixture that marks Cuba's history. The presentation sparked an exchange with audience members on differences between Cuba and Equatorial Guinea on marriage traditions and responsibility for children, attitudes toward interracial marriage, and the forging of the Cuban nation.

Other special presentations included one by the Spanish Cultural Center in Malabo, another by the Pauline Sisters staffing the literature table of the San Pablo publishing house, and another on the transformation of education in Equatorial Guinea and in Cuba today.

Hunger for books

The hunger for books among youth and other participants in the fair was evident at the literature tables. At the Cuban publishers' stand, staffed by some of the half-dozen Cuban internationalist volunteers who teach at the National University here, students eagerly picked up books and pamphlets by authors ranging from José Martí and Ernesto Che Guevara to novelist Alejo Carpentier and poet Nancy Morejón.

At the Pathfinder stand, the titles most in demand, in addition to *From the Escambray to the Congo*, were collections of speeches by Thomas Sankara, the leader of the 1983–87 popular democratic revolution in the West African country of Burkina Faso. Dozens of copies of Sankara's *We Are Heirs of the World's Revolutions* and *Women's Liberation and the African Freedom Struggle* flew off the table—in Spanish, French, and English. Young women in particular were interested in Sankara's explanation of the struggle for women's emancipation.

Books by Nelson Mandela and about the movement that overturned the apartheid regime in South Africa were equally popular, followed by *Malcolm X Talks to Young People* and *Habla Malcolm X* (Malcolm X speaks). Students also snapped up a range of Pathfinder titles, from *Capitalism's World Disorder* by Jack Barnes to issue no. 13 of *New International* magazine, featuring the article "Our Politics Start with the World."

Altogether more than 300 Pathfinder books and pamphlets were purchased, including everything by Sankara, Mandela, and Malcolm X. To assure these titles remain available to students, Pathfinder made a donation of more than 125 books to the university, which the fair organizers said would be distributed among several libraries.

At the closing session, rector Carlos Nse Nsuga spoke with great pleasure about the book fair's resounding success. He thanked "those whose efforts made this possible," including the vice minister of education, the Cuban embassy, Pathfinder Press, and the many participating faculty members.

The event concluded with a comic skit in the campus courtyard put on by students at the law school. They enacted a trial in which one man accused another of the death of his sister in a traffic accident, claiming the accused had caused her death through *brujería* (witchcraft). With humorous exchanges in Spanish and Fang, the cast had the audience rolling with laughter and won a hearty round of applause when the defendant was acquitted.

At the end the students read a statement, saying their purpose in preparing the skit was to appeal to the government to develop a body of law to deal with the all-too-common charges of witchcraft brought before the courts. Their defense of materialism and the rule of law—versus superstition and traditions that hold back the modern development of Equatorial Guinea—was warmly received by the students and faculty in attendance.

We start with the world and how to transform it

by Mary-Alice Waters

On behalf of Pathfinder Press, I would like to express our appreciation to Carlos Nse Nsuga, the rector of the National University of Equatorial Guinea, for the initiative that has been taken by the young and vital institution he heads to organize the first national book fair of Equatorial Guinea under the banner "To read is to grow."

We want to thank the vice minister of education and the government of Equatorial Guinea for their support.

To the minister, the rector, the vice rector, the dean, the members of the organizing committee, and so many others at the university here, we say thank you for the opportunity to share this moment in history with you. It is an honor.

Pathfinder Press, which is based in the United States,

Presentation on Pathfinder Press given on the opening day of the First Equatorial Guinea Book Fair, October 17, 2005. Published originally in the Militant, *November 7, 2005.*

"We hope to underline by our presence that there are ordinary people in the United States who do not start from a desire to protect the relative wealth and abundance of resources consumed in the most economically developed countries.... We start with the world and how to transform it."

TOP: Satellite photo of earth at night starkly depicts the disparity between access to electricity in Europe, North America, and Japan as compared to most of Africa, Asia, and Latin America. BOTTOM: Contingent of Young Socialists from United States at 16th World Festival of Youth and Students in Caracas, Venezuela, 2005, carry banner opposing imperialist efforts to prevent semicolonial countries from developing modern energy sources.

accepted the invitation to participate in this event for two reasons. Most important, for us it is an opportunity to learn. Even though our presence at this book fair here in Equatorial Guinea is a first, it is not unusual. Whenever possible Pathfinder takes part in book fairs and similar cultural events not only throughout the United States, Canada, and Europe, but around the globe—from Harare to Tehran, from Guadalajara to Havana, Caracas, and Buenos Aires. What we learn from our experiences here—such as the October 12 Independence Day celebration in Evinayong marking the end of colonial rule, a visit to the port of Luba yesterday to learn another part of the history, and future, of the country, and participating in this first Equatorial Guinean book fair—will help us transmit the reality of the world in which we live more accurately and more richly through the books and pamphlets we publish.

The second reason we welcomed the invitation to participate in this exchange is that our presence here helps underline that there are ordinary people in the United States who do not start from a desire to protect the relative wealth and abundance of resources consumed in the most economically developed countries. [*Applause*] There are many, like ourselves, who understand that American and European economic development exists in substantial part because billions the world over live in crushing poverty. We start with the world and how to transform the international economic order, which is the source of this reality.

We also hope to underline by our presence that you are not alone in your efforts to transform your country. To make it part of a world in which all have access to the benefits of electricity, including the ability to read and study at night, safe water to drink, paved roads that are passable year round, and modern means of communication. The installation of each new tower extending the cell phone system here is indeed a cause for celebration.

You are not alone in your efforts to assure that health care, as well as the kind of education this university strives to assure, is accessible to all. To put it in the words of one of Pathfinder's most popular titles, *The Working Class and the Transformation of Learning*, "Until society is reorganized so that education is a human activity from the time we are very young until the time we die, there will be no education worthy of working, creating humanity."

It is to this end that Pathfinder's publishing program is organized.

The books we publish—history, sociology, philosophy, culture, politics in the modern world—are directed first and foremost at working people and youth within the United States. The largest part of these books are edited and printed in English, but more and more frequently our new titles are published in Spanish and sometimes in French as well. The growing numbers of Spanish-speaking immigrants from throughout the Americas make this a necessity, while the swelling ranks of immigrants from numerous countries of West and Central Africa are among the most eager readers of our titles in French.

To introduce Pathfinder Press to you today, I want to mention four other titles, all available here during the book fair, that are indicative of who we are.

First. *How Far We Slaves Have Come!*, which features the speech given by Nelson Mandela when he visited Cuba in 1991 to thank the Cuban people for their irreplaceable contribution to the struggle to bring down the apartheid regime of South Africa. It also includes the response to that speech by Cuban president Fidel Castro.

As Mandela expressed it on that occasion: "We in Africa are used to being victims of countries wanting to carve up our territory or subvert our sovereignty. It is unparalleled in African history to have another people rise to the defense of one of us."

The defeat of the white-supremacist South African army in the historic battle of Cuito Cuanavale,[2] for which the Cuban internationalists at the side of the Angolans were primarily responsible, said Mandela, "was a milestone in the history of the struggle for southern African liberation." And he steadfastly affirmed his admiration for "the sacrifices of the Cuban people in maintaining their independence and sovereignty in the face of a vicious, imperialist-orchestrated campaign to destroy the impressive gains made in the Cuban Revolution."

How Far We Slaves Have Come!, published in both English and Spanish, is one of Pathfinder's titles that is most widely read and used in the United States, including in university and high school classes.

Second. Pathfinder has published and kept in print for nearly twenty years (something most publishers don't do for their soon-out-of-print titles) several collections of speeches by the Burkinabè leader Thomas Sankara. In English and French we have the book *Thomas Sankara Speaks*, and smaller selections of Sankara's speeches in Spanish as well as French and English.

Without a doubt, the most popular is *Women's Liberation and the African Freedom Struggle*, Sankara's powerful speech to the women of Burkina Faso on International Women's Day, March 8, in 1987, in Ouagadougou. "The struggle of the Burkinabè women is part of a worldwide struggle of all women, and beyond that, part of the strug-

---

2. In 1988, Cuban, Angolan, and Namibian combatants defeated an invasion of Angola by the South African apartheid regime, halting it at Cuito Cuanavale and then pushing the invaders out of the country.

> "The books we publish are directed first and foremost at working people and youth within the United States."

Among the many world revolutionary leaders whose speeches and writings are published by Pathfinder Press are Nelson Mandela and Fidel Castro, seen here together in Cuba, 1991 (*top*), and Thomas Sankara, leader of popular democratic revolution in Burkina Faso, 1983–87 (*bottom*). Titles by them were among the most sought-after books at the First Equatorial Guinea Book Fair.

gle for the rehabilitation of our continent," Sankara told them.

Third. *From the Escambray to the Congo* will be presented here this afternoon by its author, who is known to many of you—Víctor Dreke, today Cuba's ambassador to Equatorial Guinea. I want to take the occasion to thank the ambassador and the compañeros of the Cuban embassy here—who have done much to support and promote this event—for the opportunity to present *From the Escambray to the Congo* for the first time in a country of Africa. It is important, because even some of you who have met and talked with Ambassador Dreke are not aware of the history of his efforts on behalf of the liberation struggles of the continent. Those efforts began some forty years ago this year, with his place as second-in-command to Ernesto Che Guevara leading the Cuban volunteers who supported the anti-imperialist struggle of the people of the Congo.

I want to add only one point. *From the Escambray to the Congo*, which also opens a window on the struggles of the Cuban people to defend their independence and sovereignty—a struggle, as we are learning, with many links to the history and battles of the people of Equatorial Guinea—is used in numerous universities in the United States and has sold widely to thousands of young people of African descent especially. It is a measure of their deep interest in their own African roots, the history and legacy of slavery, and the struggles of the peoples of their historic homelands.

Fourth. It was the thirst for this knowledge that the outstanding American leader Malcolm X was responding to some four decades ago as he addressed those whose consciousness was being profoundly transformed by the mass struggle that brought down the apartheid-like system of racist segregation in the U.S. South. In one of his most famous speeches, which Pathfinder has published in *Malcolm X on Afro-American History*, he makes a powerful appeal to Afro-Americans to learn about and take pride in their African roots and the contributions of their ancestors—whose hands were "the hands that forged civilization."

To finish, we hope that above all the presence here of Pathfinder's books and its representatives—who are ourselves indicative of the diversity of historical origins of the peoples of the U.S.—will help you have a richer comprehension of the political, historical, social, and class differentiations within the United States.

We hope we will take with us a new knowledge of your history and reality today, and will be able to communicate that to a not insignificant number of people in the United States and around the world.

And we hope the activities we will share with you in the days to come will lead to new and even richer exchanges in the future.

Cuba's experience is at your disposal

by Víctor Dreke

We would like to express our appreciation, on behalf of the Cubans in Equatorial Guinea and of the Cuban people, for the magnificent event that is taking place for the first time in this country.

In 1966 I had my first opportunity to meet Equatorial Guineans living in exile in Guinea-Conakry, whose president was compañero Ahmed Sékou-Touré. At that time I never imagined I would come here and present a book in your country, which is now free and independent.

On October 1, 2003, when I arrived here officially as Cuba's ambassador to Equatorial Guinea, we set out to do everything possible to give what little help our people and our government could offer the Guinean people and

Remarks on the opening day of the First Equatorial Guinea Book Fair by Víctor Dreke, Cuba's ambassador to Equatorial Guinea, presenting From the Escambray to the Congo: In the Whirlwind of the Cuban Revolution, *published in both Spanish and English by Pathfinder Press. Dreke's remarks were published originally in the* Militant, *December 5, 2005.*

LEFT: *From the Escambray to the Congo* by Víctor Dreke. "Don't be alarmed by the photo on the cover," Dreke told students at book fair. "I was young then, like you, and got involved in things when I was fifteen." In the photo "you see workers, peasants, and young people fighting" during the early 1960s against counterrevolutionary bands in Cuba's Escambray mountains.

BOTTOM: Working people in Havana remove plaques of U.S.-owned Bank of Boston, just nationalized by the revolutionary government, amid mass mobilization of hundreds of thousands, August 1960.

GRANMA

its government. And I personally gave this book, which is being presented publicly here for the first time, to the honorable president [Teodoro] Obiang.

It was a real joy when a few days ago, on October 12 during the celebration of the thirty-seventh anniversary of this country's independence, the president told us, "I read the book and I liked it."

Let's talk a little about this book. Don't be alarmed by the photo on the cover. Times have changed. I was young then, like you, and got involved in things when I was fifteen. I was a black kid from the barrio, a poor and humble barrio, where the houses had dirt floors. That's where I was born. The situation at that time demanded a struggle against a dictatorship, the Batista dictatorship, which you'll read about in the book.

I joined the movement, as I studied and worked, and became active in the revolutionary struggle. Time passed. I was jailed and had to leave my hometown clandestinely. I went into the mountains and joined the revolutionary forces.

In 1959 the revolution triumphed. Twenty years old at the time of this victory, I had to take on various responsibilities, which are described here in the book. The title we chose for the book is *From the Escambray to the Congo: In the Whirlwind of the Cuban Revolution*. That is because something new happened every day in the revolution. We had triumphed, but part of Batista's army still existed, even though the rest had been defeated by our troops, by the people. Every day the Cuban people were being attacked.

And, finally the U.S. government—I'll say it quietly, so no ones gets scared or is offended—landed groups of mercenaries, who took up arms in nearly all the provinces of Cuba, of which there were six at that time.

Here there are compañeros who have studied in Cuba and know that at the time it was a country of 6 million—currently 11 million—with an area of 110,000 square kilometers [42,000 square miles], a small country defending itself against that assault.

In this cover photo you can see that the people involved were workers, peasants, students, and other young people who were fighting to defend the victory of the revolution. This struggle, which defeated the mercenaries, was very important and very powerful.

In 1965 the revolution and Fidel gave me the tremendous opportunity of coming to Africa—to Congo-Léopoldville, today the Democratic Republic of Congo—to fight together with Commander Ernesto Che Guevara and a group of 130 Cuban compañeros under the leadership of the Congolese liberation movement.

In the countries where we have been—at that time, as combatants, and today assisting in the country's development—the Cuban Revolution has always adhered to and will continue to adhere to the principle that those who decide things are the citizens of that country. We have always respected the decisions of the citizens of the country we are in, and have done what they have said, whether we agreed totally or partially or not at all. That is the principle of respect for a country's national sovereignty. That is why, whatever event Cuba takes part in, we put our heart and soul into it, but when the leadership of that country makes a decision, we support it.

When we arrived in Equatorial Guinea in 2003, one of the things we thought we could help with was cultural development. We came here not just to offer experiences—we don't consider ourselves wise men or wizards. Besides, we don't like to talk about ourselves or about Cuba. We came to have an exchange and learn from you, and to say:

here is Cuba's modest contribution. Cuba's experience is at your disposal; you can do the same here or not. That is a principle of the Cuban Revolution. [*Applause*]

We are very happy today that this first book fair is taking place. We too began this way with our first book fair in Havana. Today we do the fair throughout the country. Millions of books are sold at the Cuban book fair, which is an international fair.

Some day you too will do it throughout the country. You're off to a good start, in our opinion, because you've done it with determination and held it at a center for young people.

Before the end of our first fair, we had already formed the committee for the second fair, and the call was made for the second fair. And we went on from there.

Our people, like you, like all peoples, has a historic culture. But culture is like a plant: it has to be fertilized, it must be watered in order to advance; otherwise it starts to wither. In our country, which had been ruled by capitalism for many years, we had to bring culture to the masses, and the Cuban government decided to develop culture.

But in a country of 6 million inhabitants at that time, we had half a million illiterates. The first thing we carried out was a literacy campaign so that the entire population could read.[3] Otherwise, who were the books for? Who was going to read the books? The capitalists, who were the ones who knew how to read? No. We wanted the young people to read—the future generations, everyone.

---

3. From late 1960 through 1961, the revolutionary government undertook a drive to wipe out illiteracy. Central to this effort to teach three quarters of a million Cubans to read and write was the mobilization of 100,000 young people to go to the countryside, where they lived with peasants and workers they were teaching. As a result of this drive, Cuba virtually eliminated illiteracy in one year.

So the literacy campaign was organized. And the first book published in Cuba after the revolution—100,000 copies—was *Don Quixote de la Mancha*, in March 1959. [*Applause*]

That's why I say: if we achieved that, it can be done, and we know you will be able to do it. And you can count on Cuba's help.

In the case of the Congo—which is mentioned in this book, along with other places we've been, such as Guinea-Bissau—we offered our modest participation. We lost six Cuban compañeros who died fighting in the Congo, and other compañeros gave their lives in other countries, as you know.

One of the principles of our revolution—I was telling the rector this the other day, and I'll take advantage of the opportunity to say it here. Although some day you will be far away, we remain compañeros. No matter where in the world we find ourselves, we are always compañeros.

I was also explaining this to the compañeros from Pathfinder, who have done a lot of work. It cost them great effort to produce this book because, although it may not seem so, I always find it difficult to talk about myself. But they succeeded, and I always congratulate them for that.

We've gone to many places, and now we find ourselves here in Equatorial Guinea. Here we have our doctors, agricultural experts, and educators, according to the agreements decided on by your government.

But we look forward to and are striving for the day that will come when our doctors, agricultural technicians, our support personnel will be replaced completely by compañeros from Equatorial Guinea. That is what Cuba and our teachers work for: training you to replace them.

We want you to be able to advance by yourselves. What people need, after receiving help, is to be able to develop by themselves: to have their own cadres who carry out their own decisions. That is what we did in Cuba.

This book talks about war, about various forces, and many things that have changed with the times. Today we are engaged in an ideological battle—as commander Fidel Castro puts it, a battle of ideas. What is the battle of ideas? To teach the entire world to read and write. To bring health care to the entire world. To defend the national principles of each country.

Those of you who go to Cuba to study know that when you are there you celebrate your national day. And on that day—you can ask Carmela [Oyono Ayíngono], who studied in Cuba—students dress in their traditional clothing and carry out their traditional events. Cuba is your country. We don't brainwash anyone.

And we don't take with us anything from Africa or anywhere else. From Africa we have taken back to Cuba only two things: our dead—the more than 2,000 Cubans who have perished in combat in different African countries[4]— and the hearts of the majority of Africans. [*Applause*]

But we haven't taken with us either oil or anything else. When we went to Angola we never asked for a drop of oil. We didn't go there for that. We went there because Angola needed the support of Cuban forces so that apartheid would no longer mistreat and suppress that country. And we've gone to other places because it was necessary.

Today there are more than 500 Cuban doctors in Guatemala. We haven't gone there in search of Guatemalan products, but to help Guatemalans in light of the misfortune they confront because of the consequences of Hurricane Stan. And right now Cuban doctors are heading to Pakistan, at the request of the government there, in the

---

4. See note on page 69.

wake of the earthquake.[5]

Nor did we come to Equatorial Guinea looking for anything—only your hearts, because we are brothers and sisters now and forever. It's important to state this for the youth present, because sometimes the question is asked: What are these people coming here for? To offer, alongside you, what little we have.

What joy it is to see how Equatorial Guinea progresses. It's not the Guinea I knew in 2000 when I first arrived here at the Malabo airport, under a torrential downpour, and there were no lights. I could see two compañeros there with a little light shining so we could get off the plane. That's not the Malabo airport of today. It has been developed.

And what a joy that you already have a school of medicine. Sometimes the newspapers don't talk about that. You should talk about the medical school and about the doctors that are training there, of the more than 50 sixth-year students who will soon be arriving here from Cuba. We should talk about that! Because that shows the future for Equatorial Guinea. [*Applause*]

In Cuba, at the time of the revolutionary victory, we had 6,000 doctors, and we were left with 3,000, because the "friends" who live ninety miles from us—we'll say it quietly

---

5. Cuba's medical mission to Guatemala began in 1998 following the passage of Hurricane Mitch, which killed over 200 people in Guatemala and several thousand in Honduras, Nicaragua, and other countries. In response to Hurricane Stan in October 2005, hundreds of additional Cuban doctors flew to Guatemala to provide emergency assistance to nearly half a million people. Most of them stayed in the homes of patients.

In response to an earthquake that hit Pakistan in October 2005 killing 75,000, nearly 2,000 Cuban medical personnel volunteered their services, serving largely in isolated mountainous communities and treating over a million patients.

so they won't hear; everyone knows who they are!—took 3,000 doctors from us, and left us with 3,000. Yet today we have 67,000 doctors or more.

We are pleased to say that we have nearly 20,000 doctors serving in Venezuela, and we have doctors who have gone to Guatemala. The plane could not enter Guatemala; it had to stay in Honduras because of the storm conditions. They traveled by highway and there are still doctors who have not arrived at their destination because the rivers cannot be crossed. There are 500 doctors, with their backpacks on their shoulder, who are youth like yourselves. Guatemalans who had graduated from the School of Medicine in Cuba joined the group, of course, to respond to the situation in their country.

All of this is culture. Every person uses the words of their choice, but this is culture. Culture is vast, with so many places where it is developed and ways to develop it. It's the most important thing a people have.

When a people do not have culture, they simply cannot be free. That is why we understand the statement by President Obiang when he says to you that to be a cultured people is more important than to be a people that is wealthy. It's true, it's a wealth that can never be taken from you.

I was very moved by the poem by compañera Carmela. She is part of Cuba, just as I am part of Africa.

Why am I part of Africa? Because I had the opportunity to come to Africa and to sweat alongside Africans, because I had the opportunity to carry Africans and to see Africans carrying our dead in the Congo and in Guinea-Bissau. That is why I am part of Africa, just like those of you who study in Cuba are part of Cuba. Your first country is Equatorial Guinea, but you have a little piece of Cuba in you. A piece of your heart is in Cuba, like ours is in Africa.

The young people will have a chance to read this book, and perhaps some day a meeting can be held, and we can explain more details and questions you may have here. We would like to thank you again, and to thank the rector and the organizing committee of this event, which sets an example to follow.

FROM QUESTION-AND-ANSWER PERIOD

QUESTION: Our brother Fidel Castro, in his condemnation of imperialism, always says that Cubans have "the strength of the Black man, the shrewdness of the Indian, and the *mala leche*[6] of the Spaniard. [*Laughter and applause*] Could you please comment?

DREKE: It's true we have those three things. The Indians lived in Cuba, but they disappeared, because those who say they discovered us in 1492 wiped out all the Indians. Those who invaded us and colonized us—fortunately, or unfortunately—were the same ones who colonized you.[7]

And what have Blacks given us? Everything. On October 10, 1868—that's one of the reasons this month of October is important—Cubans rose up in arms against the Spanish colonial government. The leader of this revolt was Carlos Manuel de Céspedes, and together with them a large group of slaves rose up. Céspedes gave freedom to the slaves. They were the Black Africans that had been sent to Cuba in those years. So they united. That is the strength

---

6. A colloquial phrase (literally "bad milk") that in Equatorial Guinea means "orneriness."

7. The history of the two Spanish colonies are interrelated. Beginning in 1866 the colonial authorities used the island of Bioko in Equatorial Guinea (formerly known as Fernando Poo) as a penal colony for hundreds of Cuban political prisoners.

of the Blacks that we have.[8]

And our *"mala leche"*—we have to say it as you do; in Cuba this is a vulgar term but here it seems it's not, so the female compañeras will excuse us for using this phrase—our *"mala leche"* is because for years we've had to confront imperialism. In 1902, when they say we became free and independent, we were not free. They imposed on us what was called the Platt Amendment, a law that gave the U.S. government the power to intervene in Cuba any time they wanted. We had to rebel against this.

Later they installed their puppets, Batista and others before Batista. Until January 1, 1959, when the revolution triumphed, with Fidel Castro at the head. And ever since the victory of the revolution, they have wanted to crush us. We are respectful, but we will never let anyone crush us, nor are we going to sit by with our arms folded. Now things have changed and it's with books . . . But if not—and I hope not—then . . . Well, I don't want to say a lot, because later they'll say I'm leading a subversive action here. [*Laughter and applause*]

Today we continue to stand up to more than four decades of a total blockade. Despite all that, whatever we have the means to do, we will do with you.

We must defend ourselves, just as you defended yourselves in March of last year from the attempted coup by the mercenaries.[9] It so happens we live near a country

---

8. From 1868 to 1898 Cubans waged a series of wars for independence from Spain. The first, the Ten Years War, lasted from 1868 until 1878, followed by the "Little War" in 1879–80. The final war for independence was fought from 1895 to 1898, leading to the end of Spanish colonial rule. It was immediately followed, however, by a U.S. military occupation of the country.

9. In March 2004 an attempted coup against the government of Equatorial Guinea was aborted when British, South African, and other mer-

that you know . . . We said we weren't going to talk about politics. [*Laughter*] Those involved in the conspiracy were South Africans, the South Africans who are not our friends. Those in power, like Nelson Mandela, are different. They are our friends. But there are others who the Angolans and Cubans defeated at Cuito Cuanavale, where we took away their reputation for being tough guys and for being the best army in the world after the Americans.

And it's possible the South Africans involved in that conspiracy against you, had they succeeded, might have taken it out on the poor little Cubans who are here, the Cuban doctors who aren't soldiers and who don't have any guns; we don't even have knives.

They would have had to kill us. Those South Africans might come, not only to take it out on the government of Equatorial Guinea, but to take the opportunity to take it out on the little Cubans who are here. They would say: "Those were the ones who made us run in Angola." Yes sir, they sure did run—with the Angolans chasing them, and we were there next to the Angolans! That's the truth.

So the *mala leche* is for the enemy. For everyone else it's hearts and flowers.

---

cenaries were arrested in both Zimbabwe and in Equatorial Guinea. In June 2008 British mercenary Simon Mann was convicted and sentenced by an Equatorial Guinean court to thirty-four years in prison for his role in the plot in which Mark Thatcher, son of former British prime minister Margaret Thatcher, was also implicated.

> "We in Africa are used to being victims of countries wanting to carve up our territory or subvert our sovereignty," said Nelson Mandela, thanking Cuba for its aid to the liberation struggle in Angola and other African countries. "It is unparalleled in African history to have another people rise to the defense of one of us."

TOP: Cuban internationalist combatants building road in Angola, 1988, to enable troop convoys to pursue offensive that drove apartheid South Africa's invading troops out of the country. This victory helped bring a rapid end to the white supremacist regime. **BOTTOM:** Rally in Durban, South Africa, 1991, during revolutionary upsurge that toppled apartheid.

PART IV

Reporter's notebook

At time of Cuba's three wars of independence from Spain between 1868 and 1898, the island of Bioko (formerly called Fernando Poo) was used by Madrid as a penal colony for Cuban freedom fighters.

PHOTO: Cuban ambassador Víctor Dreke and Mary-Alice Waters in 2008 beside plaque in port of Malabo: "In memory of the Cubans deported to Fernando Poo in the 19th century."

Reporter's notebook

by Mary-Alice Waters

Throughout both two-week trips to Equatorial Guinea, in 2005 and 2008, Mary-Alice Waters kept a daily log of activities and observations, recorded in the form of letters to the leadership of the Socialist Workers Party.

Many of the events she wrote about were later incorporated into the Militant *articles included here. Other entries expanded on those activities, or took up aspects of the trip that went beyond the scope of the articles prepared for the newsweekly.*

The excerpts from Waters's daily reports are published here for the first time.

Her letters often refer to "we." The delegation in 2005 also included Arrin Hawkins, Martín Koppel, Jonathan Silberman, and Brian Taylor; in 2008 the other members of the delegation were Martín Koppel, Omari Musa, and Brian Taylor.

OCTOBER 2005

October 10, 2005

A number of compañeros were waiting for us at the airport in Malabo when we arrived and moved us with dispatch through customs and immigration. The welcoming crew included [Cuban ambassador to Equatorial Guinea Víctor] Dreke and [First Secretary of the Embassy] Ana [Morales]. They loaded everything into a couple of vans and SUVs and took us to the very comfortable house where we will be staying as guests of the university. After we toasted the beginning of our visit, we all piled into the SUV with Dreke and Ana for an initial tour of Malabo.

～

This morning we went to the National University of Equatorial Guinea, to meet with the vice rector and dean of the Malabo campus. They told us there are about 400 students enrolled in university classes here this year.

The vice rector, Trinidad Morgades, is a linguist whose native tongue is Pidgin English. We had a very interesting discussion with her. She described Pidgin as a language "of contact" that was born out of the history of slavery, in this case contact between the people of what is today Sierra Leone and the British, who brought slaves from that region to what is today Equatorial Guinea. She wanted to be sure we understood that the slave trade was not only between Africa and the New World, but within Africa as well. On the linguistic front, she drew the parallel to what are today the so-called Romance languages of Western Europe, which were born out of the subjugation of the peoples of those regions by the Latin-speaking Roman Empire and the homogenization of those peoples through resistance to that subjugation. What a pleasure it was to get an introduction to Equatorial Guinea from her!

She was surprised to learn that we've come from the United States and the United Kingdom to participate in the book fair. When the meeting began, she thought we were all Cubans, and said she didn't know there were people like us within the United States who defended the Cuban Revolution. We were somewhat taken aback, too, but everyone laughed and recovered.

We leave early tomorrow morning flying to Bata on the mainland, and will travel by road to Evinayong on Wednesday for the Independence Day celebration, about a three-hour trip, we're told.

October 12, 2005

The flight to Bata was about forty minutes. It was one of a number of special charters carrying diplomatic and government personnel as well as others going for the Independence Day celebration.

This evening we were the dinner guests of a businessman in Bata—a Guinean who is "in love with Cuba," as he told us.

The abounding contradictions—for us—are enlightening. In the course of the evening he proudly and laughingly told us about his fourteen kids and four or five wives. He joked that one of his daughters has announced that when she gets married, she isn't going to accept a husband with other wives. He was clearly proud of her, but said she just doesn't understand yet. Then again, maybe he doesn't see what's coming quite as well as she does.

This businessman has made a couple trips to Cuba, traveling all over there and signing a number of business deals. He said he wishes Equatorial Guinea could get an "injection of Cuban blood"—to increase discipline and *alegría*

[joy]. He spoke admiringly and appreciatively about the Cuban doctors and teachers in Equatorial Guinea and elsewhere in Africa. I asked him what made him start looking more closely at Cuba, and he responded by telling us he had been in school here when independence was won in 1968. Not long afterwards, all the teachers, who were mostly Spaniards belonging to various Catholic orders, quit the country, leaving students like himself with no way to continue their education. When Cuba began to send teachers in 1972, education resumed, but the "method" was different, he said, and that's what attracted him toward Cuba.

He is a Fang, one of the major Bantu population groups in Equatorial Guinea, Gabon, and Cameroon. He commented on the absurdity of the borders drawn by the imperialist powers, ignoring the real trade routes and tribal and linguistic ties. Fang, he said, isn't taught in schools and virtually nothing is written in Fang (except for the Bible, which has been translated by Catholic missionaries), but it's the language used at home and in daily life, the only language of many.

Bata seems like a much bigger city than Malabo, teeming with street life. The legacy of European colonization appears weaker; Spain took full control of the Continental Region only in 1926. The majority of the population of Equatorial Guinea lives here on the mainland.

Manaña off to Evinayong at 6:00 a.m.

October 14, 2005

The first hour of the trip from Bata to Evinayong was on a paved road, climbing east up and over the coastal mountains. The second two hours were on a reasonably well-graded dirt (sometimes mud) road heading south and a little east to Evinayong, the capital of the Central-

South province. They have been working on widening that section of the road for about five months, in preparation for paving it. Evinayong has a population of somewhere around 35,000, we are told.

On the way south we drove by Monte Alen, one of the few tourist destinations here. We could see the lodge from the road. Westerners come to look for mountain gorillas and other endangered flora and fauna. One of the Guinean press officials traveling with us had earlier commented with some bitterness about the large numbers of non-Africans who come here asking to see forest elephants. "Everyone comes here asking about elephants," he remarked. "But what about us?" The anti-imperialist hatred surfaces in many forms.

~

The Independence Day celebrations have been going on for several days, and the march in Evinayong was the final event.

The three-hour parade itself was quite interesting. Contingent after contingent came by, starting with the different military services, including the navy, national security units, and cadets of the different services—with helicopters overhead. There were a few women in each contingent, with more among the cadets. The military contingents were followed by several formations of very spirited *"esposas de los militares"* [wives of military personnel].

(We have no independent way of judging, but one point often made here is the importance of the military as a factor of national unity, incorporating all tribes and clans.)

The women's contingents throughout the parade were among the most interesting. They reminded me of the picture on the front cover of Pathfinder's book with Thomas Sankara's speech on women's emancipation and the Af-

The Independence Day parade in Evinayong, October 12, 2005.
TOP: "A large contingent of construction workers marching in blue work jumpsuits and white hard hats" were harbingers "of a proletariat being born." **BOTTOM:** The numerous large contingents of women were "far and away the most lively and confident."

rican freedom struggle. Organized by province and city, each of the women's association contingents wore skirts or dresses made of the same cloth, and each contingent's clothes were of a different print. They were far and away the most lively and confident, chanting and singing and dancing as they went by the reviewing stand. (I asked someone where the cloth comes from and didn't get a clear answer. There is no cotton grown in Equatorial Guinea and no textile factory, but cloth is produced in several former French West African countries such as Cameroon, Gabon, and Senegal.)

Among the largest contingents were those representing the governing party, the PDGE (Democratic Party of Equatorial Guinea), organized town by town. Other parties that belong to the government coalition marched under their own banners too. There were also contingents of youth and children's organizations. The First Lady, Constancia Mangue de Obiang, is their godmother.

The final contingents were Guinean employees of the various international companies that are the center of the oil industry, and other companies involved in building the roads and ports and other components of the infrastructure necessary to sustain the current level of foreign capitalist operations. There were contingents of employees from all the oil companies. This included ExxonMobil, Chevron, Amerada Hess, Marathon, etc.; the phone company, which is French-owned; the gas and electricity company (not sure who the major owner is); a large contingent of construction workers marching in blue work jumpsuits and white hard hats carrying huge banners depicting the hotels and government buildings they are putting up and apartment complexes that are planned. These are being built by construction companies from the People's Republic of China. Among all of these contingents, I saw only three white faces.

Aside from the women's association, I would say these contingents of workers were the proudest and most confident. Working-class organization is illegal, as are strikes, yet there are initial signs of a proletariat being born!

Everyone tells us there are very few Guineans working on the oil rigs, which is not surprising. But winning a job working at Punta Europa, as the American enclave and industrial park near Malabo is called, or with any of the foreign companies is highly prized—for pay, training, and other opportunities that open up. Undoubtedly it is those with the highest educational levels who get these jobs. On the plane coming back from Bata yesterday, various of us talked with several Guineans who had been in Evinayong marching as part of these contingents of workers—one in construction, two in oil and natural gas, and a fourth who works for the electrical company. The electrical worker told Martín he had lived in Spain for twenty-two years, in the U.S. for a while—in Los Angeles, I think—and is now back here.

Leading up to the October 12 Independence Day celebration, a lot of importance was given to the inauguration of a new GSM cell phone tower in the town of Nsork-Mbatung in the southeast region of the country; the town was also celebrating some newly paved streets and street lighting. That comes as no surprise, but it is still worth noting. Plans for electrification of the country using hydroelectric generation are on the drawing boards, in cooperation with Cameroon and Gabon, we're told. Driving from Bata to Evinayong is like a rolling panorama of "Our Politics Start with the World."[1] No electricity, except that produced by a few small

---

1. The back cover of *New International* no. 13, whose lead article is "Our Politics Start with the World" by Jack Barnes, is built around a satellite photograph of "Earth at Night," starkly depicting the disparity between

local generators. Numerous Guineans have pointed out to us the contrast between Punta Europa, which from afar at night looks like a modern imperialist city where the lights never go out—and the city of Malabo across the bay, with unpaved streets in darkness and frequent blackouts. The second striking thing was the absence of cultivated plots of land in the countryside. Quite literally, we passed not a single one in six hours of driving through rural areas. We've asked numerous people and all confirm that's the case. The diet staples, we've been told, are plantains, malanga, and the tuber that we know as yucca, which grow with little effort. People plant a tree here and there, or put a few cuttings in the ground nearby, keep a few goats or occasionally chickens in the yard, hunt monkeys and other small forest animals, and catch fish. The markets in Bata and Malabo, where the majority of the population lives, are full of people selling very small quantities of such foods—a dozen malanga or onions, no one has much. Yet many foodstuffs are extremely expensive. In Malabo we bought an onion, imported from Cameroon, for the equivalent of a dollar. And our Guinean driver assured us we were not paying a tourist premium.

We thought we were going to have part of a day to see something of Bata before returning to Malabo, but the charter we were on left in the morning. The flight crew were Afrikaans-speaking South Africans who made all safety—and other—announcements in English only!

October 15, 2005

Dreke and Ana accompanied us to meet with Carlos Nse Nsuga, rector of the National University of Equatorial

---

electrical usage in the imperialist countries of Europe and North America, and those of Asia, Africa, and Latin America. See photo on page 84.

In 1965, says Víctor Dreke, "the Cuban Revolution and Fidel Castro gave me the tremendous opportunity of coming to Africa to fight together with Commander Ernesto Che Guevara and a group of 130 Cuban compañeros under the leadership of the Congolese liberation movement."

TOP: Left to right, Fidel Castro, Víctor Dreke, and Che Guevara (in disguise), as Guevara and Dreke were leaving for Congo to support anti-imperialist forces, April 1965. Photo appears on the back cover of *From the Escambray to the Congo*. BOTTOM: Dreke (*left*) and Guevara (*right*) in Congo several months later, together with Cuban doctor Rafael Zerquera.

Guinea. Much of the discussion centered on his questions about why people in the U.S. would be interested in Cuba or Africa. Dreke gave a very good presentation on Cuba's proletarian internationalist policies in Africa over more than four decades.

When I gave the rector a copy of Dreke's book, *De la Sierra del Escambray al Congo*, the back cover photo attracted his attention. He recognized Che Guevara and Fidel Castro. "But who is the Black guy?" he asked. "That's me!" replied Dreke. From the expression on the rector's face, I think he really hadn't known. He asked Dreke many questions about his evaluation of what happened in the Congo in 1965 and why.

The rector told us he was trained as a teacher and an aviation engineer, studied in Equatorial Guinea under the Spanish when it was still a colony, and then in the Soviet Union. He contrasted the two, saying that the imperialists are always trying to encourage you—even recruit you—to leave your country of origin. In the Soviet Union they were encouraged to return and use their education to the benefit of their people.

October 17, 2005

The opening of the book fair today couldn't have been better.

The half-hour opening program started at 11:00 a.m. On the platform were the rector Carlos Nse Nsuga; Joaquín Mbana, the vice minister of education (who will be presenting a book tomorrow); Ambassador Víctor Dreke from Cuba; Hwangbo Ung Bom, the ambassador from the Democratic People's Republic of Korea; Pedro Ndong Asumu, the vice rector of the Bata branch of the university; Trinidad Morgades, the vice rector of the Malabo branch; and the poet Carmela Oyono Ayíngono, who set the tone on the importance of books and reading and extended a special welcome to the visitors from across the sea.

After a half-hour break during which all the students sat and waited, the second session began. There were about 200 in attendance, with every seat taken and the aisles full. Many were secondary school students who were listening like there was no tomorrow. The rector, vice rector, Dreke, Ana Morales, and I were on the stage, and the opening presentation was mine on Pathfinder. It was well received. I was interrupted once with an applause that took me by surprise—when I said we were there to underline that there *are* people like us in the United States who start with the world and not with protecting the relative wealth and abundance of resources consumed in the most economically developed countries.

The women—mostly university professors—who are the core of the organizing committee for the book fair were really happy by the end of the session. Perhaps it was partly because they liked the quotes I had from Sankara's speech on the women of Africa. But that was not the only thing. I never got so many hugs and double-cheeked kisses before in my life. From that point on, all the tension began dissipating, and there were smiles everywhere for the rest of the day.

The next part of the program was a brief presentation of an excellent book on the history of Equatorial Guinea by Rosendo-Ela Nsue Mibui. The author's son, Rosendo-Ela Baby, a businessman who is the vice president of the Malabo Chamber of Commerce, made the presentation as a stand-in for his father, who was in Bata.

Víctor came next. He gave a very good presentation and, to much laughter, kept apologizing for stepping outside the diplomatic protocol box. People loved it. We have it on tape and will want to run excerpts, at least, in the *Militant*.

The program ended around 1:00 p.m. After a lunch break, the tables opened again for sales until 5:00. We've rarely seen such thirst for the books. We probably sold 80 to 100 titles, including one copy or more of everything we had on the table. We rationed things to be sure to have some for the other days. Otherwise almost everything we have by Mandela and Sankara would have been gone.

There are four Cuban professors at the campus here in Malabo. One said he was really taken by surprise—pleasantly so—to see the response. He hadn't expected it. (We had. Its degree was the only question, and an important one.) Several of them told us they'd known about Pathfinder in Cuba but had never gotten to one of the book fairs. They had to come to Equatorial Guinea to finally see our books.

Several of the students who are here as part of an exchange program organized by Arcadia University near Philadelphia came by the table. They were unhappy to learn they had missed the program in the morning. They had heard it was going to begin at 6:00 p.m. One student saw *New International* no. 13 on the table with the lead article, "Our Politics Start with the World"—and told us he had bought it at the *Los Angeles Times* book fair! The experience here has had a big impact on him.

What a day! It's like watching our program come alive!

October 18, 2005

The book fair continued to go well today, with two very good presentations by Guineans, and a presentation by Ray García, the attaché at the Cuban embassy, on the "History of the Book Fair in Cuba."

One of the Guinean presentations, "Folklore as an Instrument of Education and Culture," was given by Rosalía Andeme, a professor at the university and one of the women on the organizing committee for the book fair. She explained the origins of some of the Guinean dances and music in the resistance to the slave traders and colonial oppression, and argued for students and other youth in Equatorial Guinea to embrace their cultural heritage rather than be ashamed of it.

The other Guinean presentation was by Joaquín Mbana, the vice minister of education who had opened the book fair yesterday. He has contributed to a book titled *De boca en boca* (By word of mouth), which is about Bantu folk beliefs. There were a lot of things that none of us got, since Mbana was referring to many customs and superstitions we are unfamiliar with, using names and terms in Fang we don't know. But to the extent I could follow it, he seemed to be introducing some basic materialism with a great deal of humor and ability to communicate. (Despite the fact that he said he didn't agree with those who try to give everything a material basis. Mbana studied in East Germany. Whatever Stalinist negation of "materialism" he was taught there was undoubtedly missing the dialectics.)

The most interesting thing that came up in the discussion, on how the Cuban book fair has grown from its very modest beginnings, was raised by a student who didn't understand the content of Ray's references to the educational/cultural revolution in Cuba over the years. The student identified the term "revolution" with something bad, not good, and it took a couple of rounds to clarify.

This has a lot to do with the post-independence history of Equatorial Guinea and the legacy of Stalinism in Africa (and the world). It is one of the reasons there was initially some nervousness over some of the Pathfinder titles we had brought, especially anything that had the word "revo-

lution" on the cover, because that's the word Macías used
to describe his Pol Potist dictatorship.

October 19, 2005
We underestimated the thirst for anything by Mandela.
The apartheid regime was defeated more than fifteen years
ago. It was evident that many students know little about it
concretely and are eager to get their hands on material that
brings that victory to life for them, especially writings by
Mandela, who they look to—rightly—as one of the great
leaders of the people of Africa. In deciding the relative
quantities of books we brought for the book fair here, we
were too influenced by the fact that the Spanish editions of
Nelson Mandela: Intensify the Struggle, and *How Far We
Slaves Have Come!* are titles we sell very few of today in
the United States and other non-African countries, including Latin America. Along with various Sankara books and
From the Escambray to the Congo by Víctor Dreke, *How Far
We Slaves Have Come!* was the title we brought the largest
quantities of. But we still had nowhere close to what we
should have brought.

~

I didn't have time 'til now to write about our trip to Luba.
Luba is on a magnificent, deepwater bay about half-way
down the Atlantic side of the island of Bioko. It is an hour-
plus drive from Malabo over a largely dirt road. Like the
road to Evinayong, it is being paved. Right now, Luba is
still a small, slow-moving port town. We were there on a
Sunday, and dozens of women were doing the laundry on
the rocks of the fresh water stream running through the
town, as the kids played and bathed.
According to the book *Macías: verdugo o víctima* [Macías:
executioner or victim] by the current Equatorial Guinean

ambassador to Britain that was presented during the book fair, the Soviet Union turned Luba into a major base for their Atlantic fishing fleet during the decade of the Macías dictatorship. Using dragnets that devastated the fish stock, they very profitably caught and exported large quantities of fresh seafood. In exchange, they provided the Guineans with fish that had been frozen for so many years it no longer met international standards for human consumption; it was fit only for fish meal for animal feed and fertilizers. There were reportedly severe medical reactions and some deaths, especially among children who consumed it.

One more horrifying, concrete example of the legacy of Stalinism.

~

Most interesting is what is happening in Luba right now.

Our first stop was the headquarters of Luba Freeport Ltd., where we met Howard McDowall, a Scotsman from Aberdeen who said he is in charge of the ten-year, $150 million project to transform Luba into a port through which will flow virtually all the materials needed by the imperialist enterprises engaged in oil extraction in West Africa—from Angola, to Equatorial Guinea, to Gabon, to Nigeria, to anywhere else oil is discovered. We stood on the bluff overlooking the bay as we were shown the roads and wharves being built, the landfill, where warehouses will be constructed, etc. We were told they will use the fifty-meter-deep bay to tow in and repair oil platforms. "Come back in two years and you will not recognize this place," McDowall said.

Building such a strategic center on an offshore island undoubtedly makes it less vulnerable than on the continent, where it is more easily accessible to the masses of exploited humanity whose proletarian consciousness is being born. One more glimpse of uneven and combined development here.

In the colonial period Luba was the center of cocoa production and export to Europe. Tens of thousands of Nigerians were brought in to work the plantations. (I was struck by the evidence that, similar to most of the native peoples of the Americas, the largely preclass, preagriculture, hunting and gathering Bantu population of central Africa simply could not be forced to work—at least not 'til they were forcibly separated from their homelands and societies. It's probably one reason why slaves were taken from the regions of West Africa to the north where labor productivity and class divisions were more advanced and brought to this part of Africa—as Trinidad Morgades described to us—as well as transported to the Americas.) The cocoa (and coffee) production collapsed in the 1970s, probably due to a number of factors including falling commodity prices, the extreme brutality of the dictatorship and international isolation of Equatorial Guinea, devaluation of the currency (the CFA franc) and competition from more productive cocoa cultivation in Nigeria and other countries. I've also read that the Nigerian government was trying to bring down the Macías dictatorship in hopes of picking up the pieces. There was a mass exodus of Nigerian workers. It was part of the economic devastation of the Macías period. As we drove through the rural area around Luba, abandoned cocoa plantations were evident everywhere. The bushes just grow wild, with some minimal picking of cocoa pods by isolated individual families.

The trip to Luba also gave us a chance to meet and talk with some of the Cuban medical volunteers.

Over and over again, everyone affirms that malaria is the most pervasive medical problem here. A month ago the rate of infection was very high, we were told. Right about then Marathon Oil paid for a massive fumigation sweep on Bioko (perhaps in the Continental Region too; I don't think we asked), and the incidence of malaria has fallen sharply in the last few weeks. We've been struck by how few mosquitoes we've seen, but I guess our timing was lucky. The weather has also been relatively cool, with cloudy skies and rain most days. Everyone tells us that will change when the dry period begins in a week or two, and the brutal heat will be with them until next May. (One of the Cuban doctors told us later that they don't think fumigation with DDT is a good method. The toxic residue causes other illnesses, especially among children. They favor biological controls that wipe out the larvae, a method that's safer, more effective, and longer-lasting. But that takes a different level of labor productivity and social organization. In the meantime, it is DDT that saves many lives.)

There was a serious cholera epidemic in Malabo last February. It spread to a few other centers but was fairly rapidly contained, in large part due to the effective efforts of the Cuban medical team. Other major health problems include AIDS, which is not as bad here as in many other countries of Africa but is serious and growing; violence against women; and alcoholism ("Beer is 50 cents a can; a bottle of water is $3," we were told. "Go figure.")

October 22, 2005

On the last day of the book fair, after the closing session, we all went outside to watch an excellent skit put on by a group of law students at the university. The vice minister of education, the rector, everyone was there. The skit, which lasted about forty-five minutes, was built around an accusation brought by one man against another, who he charged with killing his sister in an automobile accident.

All parties agreed that the person driving the car that caused the accident in which the sister died was someone entirely different. But the accuser insisted the real cause of his sister's death was witchcraft practiced by the accused, a *brujo* (witch), who should be sentenced to death. A lot of the allusions, references, and dialog, which had the students and faculty laughing so hard they were in tears, went over our heads. A good bit was in Fang and Bubi, the two most widely spoken African languages. But the gist was clear: materialism and the rule of law versus superstition and social relations rooted in preclass society that hold back the modern development of Equatorial Guinea. The defense attorney won a hearty round of applause for his closing statement on behalf of the accused, and the judges acquitted him. When the entire cast took a bow, they read a statement. Their motive in preparing the skit, they said, was to appeal to the government to develop a body of law, to be consistently applied, related to accusations of witchcraft. Everyone assured us the skit reflected what continues to happen in Guinean life and in the courts today.

Among the characters in the skit, the police officer, dressed in camo, a black beret, heavy military boots, and sunglasses, was portrayed as a corrupt, vicious brute, an expression of the popular hatred of the police, which we've seen and heard ample evidence of.

The whole skit was quite impressive, and really well done. The presiding judge was a woman moreover! (Of the several hundred students on the Malabo campus, around thirty are women, we were told.)

∾

Another interesting discussion took place following the presentation made by Jassellys Morales, the third secre-

MARTÍN KOPPEL/MILITANT

ARRIN HAWKINS/MILITANT

TOP: Opening of book fair, October 17, 2005. On platform, from left: university rector Carlos Nse Nsuga; Pedro Ndong Asumu, vice rector of Bata campus; Cuban ambassador Víctor Dreke; Hwangbo Ung Bom, ambassador from North Korea; and Trinidad Morgades, vice rector of Malabo campus.

BOTTOM: On last day of fair, law students performed well-received skit appealing for development of a body of law to deal with charges of witchcraft brought before the courts.

tary at the Cuban embassy, on "La mujer negra en la literatura y las artes plásticas del siglo XIX en Cuba" [Black women as depicted in literature and art in 19th century Cuba]. When I saw that title on the program I wondered what it could possibly be. It turned out to be a very informative presentation on slavery, sexual relations, marriage, and the racial mixture that is part of the forging of the Cuban nation. (I certainly learned a number of things I didn't know.) The issues that were raised touch on a very controversial question in Equatorial Guinea, where mixed couples on the street immediately draw hostile remarks and more. We learned that firsthand as we moved around during our two-week visit.

After Jassellys gave her presentation, the first question was, "In Cuba today, if a child is born to a woman who is not married, to whom does it belong?" Jassellys started answering as you would expect, explaining that a child does not belong to either the man or woman, that men are obligated by law to acknowledge paternity and that both parents are economically and socially responsible for the child. The rector raised his hand and asked for the microphone, saying he thought he should clarify the question being asked. In Equatorial Guinea, he explained, "we have two forms of marriage. One was imposed on us by the colonial powers. The other is our own customs. Among the Fang, to whom a child belongs depends on whether a bride price has been paid by the man to the woman's family. If it has, from that time on, any child born to the woman belongs to the man, no matter who the father is. If no bride price has been paid, the child belongs to the woman's tribe and clan. That is what the student is asking about."

Engels's *The Origin of the Family, Private Property, and the State* came marching on the stage! (And not for the first time since we've been here!)

Discussion on the second question was just as fascinating. A student asked about sexual relations between blacks and whites in Cuba and whether that is accepted. Jassellys, who is a mulatta, reiterated some of the points made in her initial presentation. She then talked about her own family, pointing out that her husband is "white," and as for her parents, grandparents, brothers and sisters, cousins, and uncles and aunts, they are every shade in the spectrum, from very dark to very light. "That's just the reality of who Cubans are," she noted. "We are not of different 'races,' just of different skin colors."

October 25, 2005

Prior to the formal closing, the last day of the book fair included a couple sessions of poetry readings, presentation of a novel by a writer from the island of Annobón, and a session on "The Cultural Revolution in Equatorial Guinea and Cuba." The latter was a presentation on education in Guinea today compared to pre-independence days, given by a professor at the university, and quite a good presentation by Ana [Morales] on the Battle of Ideas in Cuba today.

Two things about Equatorial Guinean history are striking. Prior to independence, of course, education was totally dominated by the Catholic Church. At least one person noted that the only books they ever got were catechisms. This was still a colony of Franco's clerical-fascist Spain. The governor of South Bioko province told us he had been organized into a pro-Franco youth group as a child. Eradicating those Falangist-tinged traditions in Equatorial Guinea is part of the effort to develop post-independence organizations and social relations.

The other point was the devastating impact of the departure of all the teachers after independence, as the violence of the Macías dictatorship was unleashed not only against foreigners but also against virtually anyone in the country with an education. As we had been told early on during our visit, it was only with the arrival of volunteer teachers from Cuba in the early 1970s that a nonclerical, postindependence school system began to be created. There was no university until 1995.

October 26, 2005

Wednesday evening we were invited to attend a meeting of the Malabo Rotary Club at which Leonardo Ramírez, the head of the Cuban medical collaboration in Equatorial Guinea, was the speaker. Leonardo made a presentation on what it would take to organize "Operación Milagro"[2] in Equatorial Guinea, similar to the program now being carried out in Venezuela and elsewhere in the Caribbean.

In Equatorial Guinea, the proposal of the Cuban medical brigades is to procure a bus that can be outfitted as a rolling laser eye-surgery clinic to move around the country and perform the estimated 3,000 operations that would wipe out blindness due to cataracts and related vision problems in a matter of a few months. The entire project, they estimate, would cost only $100,000, plus the price of the bus.

---

2. Operación Milagro [Operation Miracle] was established in 2004 through an agreement between Cuba and Venezuela, whereby thousands of Venezuelans suffering from cataracts, cataract-induced blindness, and other problems of vision treatable by laser surgery would go to Cuba for treatment, free of charge. The program was extended to other countries, and soon the operations began being carried out by Cuban doctors working not in Cuba but in the countries of origin of the patients. By the beginning of 2008, Operación Milagro was under way in nineteen countries. Over a million in Latin America and elsewhere have been treated.

At the meeting that night were also French diplomatic personnel, a representative of the European Union, and a number of prominent Malabo businessmen and women. The whole meeting took place going back and forth between Spanish and French, both of which most present seemed to understand without translation.

When Leonardo finished his presentation, one of the Europeans immediately asked, "You've used the figure 3,000 Guineans who need this operation. Can you give me a price for treating ten?"

I kid you not!

Leonardo was great. Without missing a beat, he politely replied that the difference in cost between treating ten people and wiping out cataract blindness in the whole country was so minimal as to be not worth discussing.

In the end, the Rotary Club set up a commission to study the proposal. Imperialist concern for humanity in action.

~

We don't have the final figures yet, but we sold close to 300 books and pamphlets, most of which were priced at the equivalent of $2 and $6, coming to about $500 in sales (minus what would have been a 20 percent commission on converting CFA francs to dollars!). We made a donation to the university of about 125,000 CFA francs (about $268). We thought it was important to do so, as we wanted to emphasize that our presence there was not a commercial undertaking. The gesture was much appreciated. As the rector put it in his remarks closing the event, "We recognize that you did not come here to take away oil. You have worked with us, asking nothing in return."

I'm sure I will remember other things later, but that's it for wrapping up this trip.

JULY–AUGUST 2008

July 28, 2008

Saturday—July 26—was our first full day here in Malabo. After breakfast we were off to the port city of Luba on the southwest coast of the island of Bioko to meet with the Cuban medical brigade there and join them for the program they had planned in celebration of the assault on Moncada.[3]

Luba is the town we visited during our trip in 2005 where a major deepwater free port is being constructed. The hope is that it can become a service center for the oil industry from Angola to the Nigerian delta, a place where major repairs on ships and deepwater drilling platforms can be done.

Unfortunately, as soon as we reached Luba we got a call saying we needed to return to Malabo fairly quickly for another meeting, so we didn't have time to tour the Freeport area. It's too bad. We were hoping to see what's changed in the last three years.

The governor of South Bioko, José Nguema Nba Nza, joined the celebration at the house where the Cuban volunteers live. He told us he first learned a little about Cuba in the early 1970s when Cuban military advisers came to

---

3. On July 26, 1953, some 160 revolutionaries under the command of Fidel Castro launched an insurrectionary attack on the Moncada army garrison in Santiago de Cuba together with a simultaneous attack on the garrison in Bayamo, opening the revolutionary armed struggle against the Fulgencio Batista dictatorship. After the attack's failure, Batista's forces massacred more than fifty of the captured revolutionaries. Fidel Castro and twenty-seven others, including Raúl Castro and Juan Almeida, were tried and sentenced to up to fifteen years in prison. They were released on May 15, 1955, after a public defense campaign forced Batista's regime to issue a general amnesty for political prisoners.

help train the new armed forces of Equatorial Guinea. There are five compañeras and compañeros in the medical brigade here, three doctors, one nurse, and a laboratory technician. (That's a medium-size brigade, we've learned. The largest are seven and the smallest are two—one doctor and one nurse. They now have medical teams working in all 18 districts of Equatorial Guinea—some 160 medical people in all.) The director of the hospital, who was also part of the celebration, is one of the Guinean doctors who graduated in 2006. That was the first class to graduate from the medical school organized by the Cubans here in Equatorial Guinea. Two other Cuban doctors who are stationed in Riaba, a small town on the west coast of South Bioko, also came over to join the activities. Juan Carlos Méndez, the head of the medical brigades for all Equatorial Guinea, told us that some such event takes place every month, allowing compañeros from several brigades to get together for political and social activity.

Saturday night we joined the July 26 celebration back in Malabo, hosted by the medical brigade there. The evening was quite an affair. There were 75–80 people in attendance, including all of the 47 Cubans in Malabo (except for those back home on vacation leave). But the crowd also included a good number of Equatorial Guineans who have studied in Cuba; five Guinean students who have just finished their premed courses and will be starting medical school in September; around ten Ethiopians, all of whom studied in Cuba during the 1980s and are now working in Equatorial Guinea; and the new Venezuelan chargé d'affaires, who remembered meeting Omari in Caracas last year.

The evening's program focused on the international fight to win freedom for Gerardo Hernández, Ramón Labañino, Fernando González, Antonio Guerrero, and René

González.[4] The presentations had more solid content than many I have heard. There were biographical sketches of each of the five—three of them given by the Guinean students just starting med school. There was a presentation on the legal issues involved, including the most recent federal appeals court decision in Atlanta, which was given by a Cuban lawyer who works with the ministry of the environment. It was quite good. They also asked me to say a few words on work being done in the United States. I took advantage of the opportunity to explain the place of the five on the front lines of the class struggle in the U.S. and their political work in the prisons. It got a good response. The evening ended with a great Cuban dinner (roast pork, of course), rum, beer, and dancing.

Sunday afternoon, before catching a flight from Malabo to Bata, we had two very interesting, if brief, meetings. One was with the Cuban electrical brigade recently arrived in Malabo—seven compañeros (all men so far) who are here to train and work with Guineans responsible for upgrading the electrical infrastructure in the country. They kept

---

4. Known as the Cuban Five, these revolutionaries were arrested and framed up in the United States in September 1998, when the FBI announced to much fanfare that it had discovered a "Cuban spy network" in Florida. After twenty-six months in federal detention, seventeen of them in solitary confinement, the five were put on trial. In June 2001 each of them was convicted on charges of "conspiracy to act as an unregistered foreign agent." Hernández, Guerrero, and Labañino were also convicted of "conspiracy to commit espionage," and Hernández of "conspiracy to commit murder." The five were given sentences ranging from fifteen years to double life plus fifteen years.

The five had accepted assignments to monitor counterrevolutionary groups in the United States planning terrorist attacks in Cuba, and keep the Cuban government informed. Their case has generated a broad international campaign to denounce the draconian sentences and harsh conditions of their imprisonment and to demand their release.

stressing over and over that their first priority is training their colleagues in safety procedures. Not hard to imagine why!

We also had a brief visit with five of the university professors (all men in this case again) who were leaving the next day for one-month vacations in Cuba. That's what everyone gets midway through their two-year commitment. They were all in good spirits, to say the least.

The all-male composition of both those groups is not representative of the overall balance of men and women among the 230 Cubans in the country. Some 59 percent of the medical brigade members are women. And women are the *jefas* of two of the four brigades we have visited so far.

July 31, 2008

We got to Bata around midnight Sunday and are staying at a nice small hotel run by a friendly, vigilant Paraguayan woman, with a staff that seems to be mostly Cameroonian and Malian. We have been speaking more French than Spanish with small shopkeepers and service personnel here!

Literally everything you buy in Equatorial Guinea is imported. Not surprisingly, a majority of small merchants seem to be immigrants too. Lebanese, Cameroonians, Senegalese, more and more Chinese, etc. Ancient trade routes, just brought into the twenty-first century with air transport and internet cafés. Construction work is carried out overwhelmingly by immigrant labor from Mali, Burkina Faso, and elsewhere in Africa. Capitalist firms from China and several Arab countries seem to be the ones that invest in the big jobs—the roads, airports, stadiums, and other government projects.

Over and over you hear the comment that these businesses—and Equatorial Guinean ones too—don't hire Equatorial Guineans because Guineans don't like to work. Whenever we get the chance, we ask, "Why should they?" None of our ancestors did either until the rising bourgeoisie forced them into the factories. There is no peasantry here that has been driven off the land and deprived of any means to survive except by selling their labor power. When we asked if land was private property in Equatorial Guinea, we were told, "sí y no." It depends on whether any individual in the rising capitalist class decides he or she wants it (as in vast parts of Europe and America at the dawn of capitalism). If not, you just stake out some ground, build a shack, plant some tubers, and hope no one bothers you. No capitalist industry has yet developed here (the only factories are a small water and juice bottling plant, a brewery, a cement factory). No land cultivation is necessary to survive—just stick a tuber in the ground and a few months later you have food. Ditto with a few banana trees. The rain forest is full of monkeys, porcupine, forest rats, and other jungle meat. The rivers and sea provide fish. There are even relatively few domesticated animals—some goats, but few pigs and even fewer chickens.

In other words, there are individual alternatives to wage slavery and debt slavery, so why work?

Pathfinder should publish George Novack's *The Long View of History* in Spanish! A historical materialist foundation for understanding the world we live in today is irreplaceable. Without it, nothing makes sense!

From early Monday morning to late Wednesday night we were on the move twelve to fourteen hours a day. We visited Cuban medical brigades in six different districts of continental Equatorial Guinea in three days. This included the towns of Ebebiyin, Mongomo, Niefang, Evinayong, Mbini, and Kogo—from the extreme northeast corner of the country to the extreme southwest. While major stretches of road we traveled had, since the last time we were here, been transformed into smooth, newly paved highways that were a pleasure to drive, there were also many, many miles of roads under various stages of construction over very difficult terrain.

The program wasn't something organized especially for us. We had the good fortune to be able to join a tour organized for the rector of the National University, the compañeros in charge of the medical brigades and medical school here, and the Cuban ambassador and first secretary of the embassy. The purpose of their tour was to evaluate the first few months of a new program that has been initiated to offer full medical school training in multiple provincial cities. This will allow students who could not otherwise overcome the financial and other barriers to entering medical school in Bata to become doctors. It is quite impressive. We basically listened in as they discussed among themselves the progress made and problems they are in the midst of trying to resolve, including the concerns some of the students had about the material shortcomings.

We learned a great deal, much of which we'll be able to work up in articles for the *Militant*.

∿

Today the French and Spanish TV news programs are full of tributes to Nelson Mandela on his ninetieth birthday, including a state banquet offered by the good Queen Elizabeth II of the United Kingdom. Mandela, as usual, had the grace and dignity to take it all in stride, although he could have been pardoned had he asked Her Royal Highness what she had done to secure his release during his nearly three decades in the prisons of apartheid!

A government official we met here told us a story that

highlights some of the real challenges. He said he was commenting to his secretary, a young, well-educated Guinean woman, about the birthday celebrations taking place around the world, and she asked, "Who is Mandela?" She didn't know. When he responded that Mandela is honored throughout the world for his leadership of the anti-apartheid struggle and his dignity in resisting twenty-seven and a half years in apartheid's prisons, she asked what he had been imprisoned for. "Was it drug trafficking?" It reminded me of how eager Guinean students were during the book fair three years ago to get their hands on *anything*, absolutely *anything*, about Mandela and the struggle to bring down the apartheid regime. Most of them weren't born yet when that history was written by the people of Africa and the workers of the world.

August 3, 2008

Yesterday we took a full day's trip about two-thirds of the way across continental Equatorial Guinea to Añisok, the district capital closest to the mountainous region of the Wele River where the hydroelectric project is under way. The river is the largest in Equatorial Guinea, we are told, and empties into the sea near Mbini where we were earlier in the week. We were welcomed by Pedro Mba Obiang Abang, the government delegate in Añisok (the elected member of parliament who belongs to the PDGE, the Democratic Party of Equatorial Guinea, which, together with some allies, has ninety-nine out of one hundred seats in the national assembly). He then drove us another thirty-five kilometers up the road that is under construction, leading to the site where the dam and hydroelectric plant will be built. We hiked a short distance down the trail running along the river to Djibloho, the spot where the water comes cascading down a steep narrow chute with great force, even now in the driest months of the year.

They started building the road on January 1. It will take almost two years to complete. But that has to be done before they can bring in much of the heavy equipment that will be needed to actually build the dam and plant. They project four to five years total before the power plant is online. It is expected to provide electricity not only for all of continental Equatorial Guinea, but for areas of Cameroon and Gabon as well. A Chinese corporation is the main contractor, but there will be several others from various countries the delegate told us. The signs at the site warning of blasting schedules, etc., were in Chinese and Spanish.

In addition to being an impressive work under way, the spot is truly beautiful!

The road to the hydroelectric generating plant-in-becoming near Añisok is being built by an Iranian enterprise. This is the first time we have run into Iranians among the many contractors from different countries working here. The skilled heavy equipment operators along the route were Iranian, though not the laborers. We stopped briefly at the compound where the Iranian workers live because the delegate wanted to talk to some of the Equatorial Guinean personnel there about coming in to Añisok for the August 3 Liberation Day activities. The Iranians greeted us with friendly waves, but we didn't get a chance to get out and talk with them.

The visit to the hydroelectric project was organized for us by Jerónimo Osa Osa Ekoro, the minister of information, culture, and tourism, who facilitated our entire trip here, including the interview with President Obiang. I doubt that many people have been taken to this site. It turns out the minister is from Añisok, and his mother warmly welcomed us in her home when we came back from the hydroelectric project. Among other things, she is the head of the women's organization in the district. Before we left, we presented her with a copy of *Women's Liberation and the African Freedom Struggle* by Thomas Sankara, which she was clearly pleased to get. We also gave the district delegate a copy of Dreke's book *From the Escambray to the Congo* in appreciation of his generous time and guided tour of the site, and left a copy of Sankara's *We Are Heirs of the World's Revolutions* with them as well.

Everything took twice as long as planned, of course, so by the time we got back to Bata we had missed the flight to Malabo that we were originally booked on. We got the last flight out, arriving in Malabo after 10:00 p.m. We had not eaten all day—except for some light snacks and drinks provided by our hosts—but one of the doctors who organizes the AIDS treatment center here in Malabo had prepared a full dinner for us that we gratefully ate around 11:00 last night. As we were enjoying her food, the doctor gave us a very rich and concrete account of the never ending *lucha* to prevent the various international drug monopolies from passing off worthless AIDS medicines on countries like Equatorial Guinea.

August 5, 2008

We just got back from the full-day program that began with the graduation ceremony for the class of 2008 from the National University of Equatorial Guinea (including twenty-one medical students), plus an event that took place in the plaza in front of the conference hall where the graduation ceremony took place. That event was really an extension of the August 3 celebration of the "Golpe de la libertad" (the coup d'état that brought down the Macías dictatorship). Obiang gave an interesting half-hour speech to an assembled crowd of a thousand or so construction workers and other members of the governing party. A whole section of it focused on the setback of the Macías period, and what it has meant for Equatorial Guinea to come back from that horrendous start as a country independent of colonial rule for the first time in almost 200 years. "Many Guineans wondered if the past hadn't been better," Obiang said. This is all a change since our visit in 2005, when the period of the Macías dictatorship was almost a taboo subject. Now people talk about it casually and as a matter of fact, saying 1979 was when Equatorial Guinea began to develop as an independent country.

The graduation ceremony was quite a manifestation of pride in accomplishments, too. There was both individual pride by students at having overcome so many obstacles to studying and earning a university degree, and collective national pride over the development of the National University of Equatorial Guinea.

The final event was a reception for all the new graduates and the university faculty at a hotel on the waterfront. Very nice.

～

On Monday in Malabo we were able to meet with Rosendo-Ela Nsue Mibui for an hour and a half. That was a real pleasure. He is the author of a substantial two-volume history of Equatorial Guinea (published in Spanish) and is widely considered the country's preeminent historian. We bought the first volume, *The History of Equatorial Guinea: Precolonial Period*, in 2005. The second volume has just been published and we are bringing it back with us. It covers the colonial period through the Macías dictatorship. (Rosendo, a veteran of the independence struggle, was imprisoned for a number of years under Macías's regime.)

~

Another of the very big infrastructure projects we visited on our way back from Mongomo last week is the new international airport that is under construction about thirty-five kilometers from there, near Mongomeyen. It is being built to act as a regional airport, serving not only Equatorial Guinea but parts of Cameroon and Gabon as well, and able to handle the largest new passenger and cargo planes. The main landing strip is partly finished, but they told us it will be another two to three years before the airport is operational. We were told that of the two large construction companies building it, one is based in Austria and the other in Brazil. This was another visit arranged for us by the minister of information. It was very useful.

August 9, 2008

A couple of compañeros picked us up this afternoon for a drive-around tour of Malabo. That activity had been on our agenda several times during the two weeks we've been here, but we'd never managed to squeeze it in. Not only is a major expansion of the deepwater port of Malabo under way, but also the historic center of the city is being restored, and an extensive new city known as Malabo II is being built from scratch. There are already a hundred or so new small houses and numerous multistory apartment buildings nearing completion. We were told they are occupied by Guinean government functionaries and by families being moved from some of the poorest areas of the city. A few of the Cuban internationalists are being housed in these areas. We were never able to get clear answers to questions we asked many different people about how one gets chosen to live in these new housing projects being built, or how much apartments or homes in them cost. But I don't think there is any mystery. Connections count.

Malabo II is being built with a modern sewage system, electrical service, plumbing that will eventually be able to distribute safe drinking water (when such becomes available), paved and lighted streets, etc. Close to that area of the city we also saw countless huge government ministries and other office buildings going up and broad new boulevards being built.

Most edifices the government builds are done in duplicate—one in Malabo and one in Bata. The ministries, national assembly, etc., sometimes meet and work in one city, sometimes in the other. All government ministers build homes in both cities, we were told, and usually in their hometowns as well.

The dual capital setup is a legacy of the country's colonial and postcolonial history. Malabo has been the longtime historic capital of the country—it was where the colonial powers ensconced themselves for centuries before they were able to dominate the Fang territories on the mainland. Historically the majority of the population on the island of Bioko is Bubi, the second-largest ethnic group in the country.[5] The Bubi (and other non-Fang tribes) were the target of fierce repression under the Macías dictatorship. Even though Bata is increasingly the commercial and political center of the country, to move the capital to the Continental Region where the majority of the population (overwhelmingly Fang, most of them speaking one or two major dialects) lives could destabilize the current national unity. Over time, of course, the economic and political weight of Bata will exert its pull. But this is not a small matter. While the Fang have dominated the govern-

---

5. See "Major populations of Equatorial Guinea" map on page 30.

ment, military, and all other centers of power since independence, posts in the ministries and national assembly are carefully distributed to maintain a certain balance among those belonging to the various tribes and clans. In speeches we have heard, Obiang has several times referred with pride to the fact that in Equatorial Guinea they have not experienced the kind of ethnic "genocide" that has torn apart not a few African countries created by the imperialist powers.

Driving around in Malabo we were all struck by the large number of Chinese workers we saw on the streets (this was late Saturday afternoon). Most of the large government construction projects are being built by Chinese companies. Guineans praise the quality of their work and especially the speed, marveling that the Chinese often work double shifts and rarely take days off. The Chinese companies bring Chinese skilled craftsmen as well as Chinese laborers.

The term for unskilled workers in Equatorial Guinea is *peón*, the old feudal designation for indentured labor. On other projects, the *peones* are generally Black from a number of African countries.

August 11, 2008

I took advantage of the long plane ride back to start digging into the second volume of Rosendo-Ela's history of the colonial and postcolonial period of Equatorial Guinea. One of the foundations of the colonial regime was the designation of every Guinean as the legal equivalent of a minor, with no rights to own property, control their own wages, enter into contracts, receive wages that they controlled, or make any decisions for himself (to say nothing of herself). Anything they "earned" for what was in fact forced labor went into an account controlled by a government-established agency and was supposed to be used to finance schools, clinics, etc., for the good of the "natives." Quite a setup!

As Fidel so aptly put it, "How far we slaves have come!"

INDEX

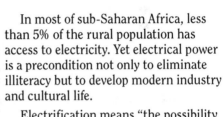

Further reading

THE COMMUNIST MANIFESTO
Karl Marx and Frederick Engels

CAPITAL
Karl Marx

To the degree capitalism develops, wrote Marx and Engels in the *Communist Manifesto* (1848), to the same degree a modern working class grows—"a class of laborers, who live only so long as they find work and who find work only so long as their labor increases capital." It is a system, wrote Marx in *Capital* two decades later, that comes into the world "dripping from head to toe, from every pore with blood and filth." *Communist Manifesto* $5, also in Spanish and French. *Capital* $18, also in Spanish.

COSMETICS, FASHIONS, AND THE EXPLOITATION OF WOMEN
Joseph Hansen, Evelyn Reed, Mary-Alice Waters

How big business plays on women's second-class status and social insecurities to market cosmetics and rake in profits. The introduction by Waters explains how the entry of millions of women into the workforce during and after World War II irreversibly changed U.S. society and laid the basis for a renewed rise of struggles for women's emancipation. $15

UNITED STATES VS. THE CUBAN FIVE
A JUDICIAL COVERUP
Rodolfo Dávalos Fernández

The story of the frame-up of five Cuban revolutionaries living in the U.S., convicted in 2001 of conspiracy to commit espionage, attempted murder, and other charges. Sentenced to federal prison terms ranging from 15 years to double life plus 15, their only "crime" was keeping tabs for the Cuban government on counterrevolutionary groups who have carried out violent attacks on Cuba from the early 1960s to today. $22

THE LONG VIEW OF HISTORY

George Novack

Revolutionary change is fundamental to social and cultural progress. This pamphlet explains why—and how the struggle by working people to end oppression and exploitation is a realistic perspective built on sound scientific foundations. $7

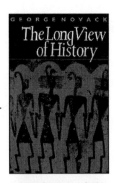

THE ORIGIN OF THE FAMILY, PRIVATE PROPERTY, AND THE STATE

Frederick Engels

How the emergence of class-divided society gave rise to repressive state bodies and family structures that protect the property of the ruling layers and enable them to pass along wealth and privilege. Engels discusses the consequences for working people of these class institutions—from their original forms to their modern versions. $18

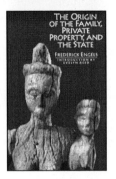

THE ESSENTIAL WORKS OF LENIN

V.I. Lenin

Contains classic works on historical materialism and revolutionary strategy: *What is to Be Done?*, *State and Revolution*, *Imperialism, the Highest Stage of Capitalism*, and excerpts from *The Development of Capitalism in Russia*. $12.95

PROBLEMS OF EVERYDAY LIFE

CREATING THE FOUNDATIONS FOR A NEW SOCIETY IN REVOLUTIONARY RUSSIA

Leon Trotsky

Articles from the early Soviet press on social and cultural issues in the struggle to forge new social relations. The advance of culture, Trotsky notes, requires an increasing level of scientific, technological, and industrial development to "free humanity from a dependence upon nature that is degrading"—a goal that can only be completed when social relationships are "free from mystery and do not oppress people." $29

African freedom struggle

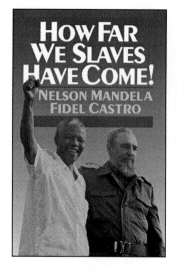

How Far We Slaves Have Come!
SOUTH AFRICA AND CUBA IN TODAY'S WORLD
Nelson Mandela, Fidel Castro
Speaking together in Cuba in 1991, Mandela and Castro discuss the place in the history of Africa of Cuba and Angola's victory over the invading U.S.-backed South African army, and the resulting acceleration of the fight to bring down the racist apartheid system. $10. Also in Spanish.

Thomas Sankara Speaks
THE BURKINA FASO REVOLUTION 1983–87
Colonialism and imperialist domination have left a legacy of hunger, illiteracy, and economic backwardness in Africa. In 1983 the peasants and workers of Burkina Faso established a popular revolutionary government and began to combat the causes of such devastation. Thomas Sankara, who led that struggle, explains the example set for Africa and the world. $24. Also in French.

Women's Liberation and the African Freedom Struggle
Thomas Sankara
"There is no true social revolution without the liberation of women," explains the leader of the 1983–87 revolution in Burkina Faso. $8. Also in Spanish and French.

The Coming Revolution in South Africa

Jack Barnes

Writing nearly a decade before the fall of the white supremacist regime, Barnes explores the social character and roots of apartheid in South African capitalism and the tasks of toilers in city and countryside in dismantling it as they forge a communist leadership of the working class. Also includes "Why Cuban Volunteers Are in Angola," two speeches by Fidel Castro. In *New International* no. 5. $14

At the Side of Che Guevara

INTERVIEWS WITH HARRY VILLEGAS (POMBO)

Villegas worked and fought alongside Ernesto Che Guevara for a decade—in Cuba, the Congo, and Bolivia. A brigadier general in Cuba's Revolutionary Armed Forces, he talks about the struggles he has taken part in over four decades and explains the importance of Guevara's political legacy for a new generation around the world. $4. Also in Spanish.

Malcolm X Talks to Young People

Four talks and an interview given to young people in Ghana, the United Kingdom, and the United States in the last months of Malcolm's life. He discusses imperialist intervention in the Congo and Vietnam, why he stopped using the description "Black nationalism," and more. Concludes with memorial tributes by a young socialist leader to this great revolutionary. $15. Also in Spanish.

Malcolm X on Afro-American History

The hidden history of the labor of people of African origin and their achievements. $11

Nelson Mandela Speaks

FORGING A DEMOCRATIC, NONRACIAL SOUTH AFRICA

Speeches from 1990–93 recounting the struggle that put an end to apartheid and opened the fight for a deep-going political and social transformation in South Africa. $25

www.pathfinderpress.com

From the Escambray to the Congo

In the Whirlwind of the Cuban Revolution
VÍCTOR DREKE

The author describes how easy it became after the Cuban Revolution to take down a rope segregating blacks from whites in the town square, yet how enormous was the battle to transform social relations underlying all the "ropes" inherited from capitalism and Yankee domination. Dreke, second in command of the internationalist column in the Congo led by Che Guevara in 1965, recounts the creative joy with which working people have defended their revolutionary course—from Cuba's Escambray mountains to Africa and beyond. $17. Also in Spanish.

Our History Is Still Being Written

The Story of Three Chinese-Cuban Generals in the Cuban Revolution

Armando Choy, Gustavo Chui, and Moisés Sío Wong talk about the historic place of Chinese immigration to Cuba, as well as over five decades of revolutionary action and internationalism, from Cuba to Angola and Venezuela today. Through their stories we see the social and political forces that gave birth to the Cuban nation and opened the door to socialist revolution in the Americas. $20. Also in Spanish.

The First and Second Declarations of Havana

Nowhere are the questions of revolutionary strategy that today confront men and women on the front lines of struggles in the Americas addressed with greater truthfulness and clarity than in these uncompromising indictments of imperialist plunder and "the exploitation of man by man." Adopted by million-strong assemblies of the Cuban people in 1960 and 1962. $10. Also in Spanish and French.

www.pathfinderpress.com

Che Guevara Talks to Young People

ERNESTO CHE GUEVARA

In eight talks from 1959 to 1964, the Argentine-born revolutionary challenges youth of Cuba and the world to study, to work, to become disciplined. To join the front lines of struggles, small and large. To politicize their organizations and themselves. To become a different kind of human being as they strive together with working people of all lands to transform the world. $15. Also in Spanish.

Playa Girón/Bay of Pigs

Washington's First Military Defeat in the Americas

FIDEL CASTRO, JOSÉ RAMÓN FERNÁNDEZ

In fewer than 72 hours of combat in April 1961, Cuba's revolutionary armed forces defeated a U.S.-organized invasion by 1,500 mercenaries. In the process, the Cuban people set an example for workers, farmers, and youth the world over that with political consciousness, class solidarity, courage, and revolutionary leadership, one can stand up to enormous might and seemingly insurmountable odds—and win. $20. Also in Spanish.

Marianas in Combat

Teté Puebla and the Mariana Grajales Women's Platoon in Cuba's Revolutionary War 1956–58

TETÉ PUEBLA

Brigadier General Teté Puebla, the highest-ranking woman in Cuba's Revolutionary Armed Forces, joined the struggle to overthrow the U.S.-backed dictatorship of Fulgencio Batista in 1956, when she was fifteen years old. This is her story—from clandestine action in the cities, to serving as an officer in the victorious Rebel Army's first all-women's unit—the Mariana Grajales Women's Platoon. For nearly fifty years, the fight to transform the social and economic status of women in Cuba has been inseparable from Cuba's socialist revolution. $14. Also in Spanish.

Dynamics of the Cuban Revolution

A Marxist Appreciation

JOSEPH HANSEN

How did the Cuban Revolution unfold? Why does it represent an "unbearable challenge" to U.S. imperialism? What political obstacles has it overcome? Written as the revolution advanced from its earliest days. $25

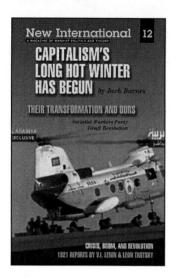

New International 12
A MAGAZINE OF MARXIST POLITICS AND THEORY

CAPITALISM'S
LONG HOT WINTER
HAS BEGUN *by Jack Barnes*

THEIR TRANSFORMATION AND OURS
Socialist Workers Party
Draft Resolution
ARABIYA
EXCLUSIVE

CRISIS, BOOM, AND REVOLUTION
1921 REPORTS BY V.I. LENIN & LEON TROTSKY

Capitalism's Long Hot Winter Has Begun
Jack Barnes

Today's sharpening interimperialist conflicts are fueled both by the opening stages of what will be decades of economic, financial, and social convulsions and class battles, and by the most far-reaching shift in Washington's military policy and organization since the U.S. buildup toward World War II. Class-struggle-minded working people must face this historic turning point for imperialism, and draw satisfaction from being "in their face" as we chart a revolutionary course to confront it. In *New International* no. 12. $16

Imperialism, the Highest Stage of Capitalism
V.I. Lenin

Imperialism not only increases the weight of debt bondage and parasitism in capitalist social relations, writes Lenin, but above all makes the competition of rival capitals—domestic and foreign—more violent and explosive. Amid capitalism's growing world disorder today, Lenin's 1916 booklet remains a foundation stone of the communist movement's program and activity. $10. Also in Spanish.

Lenin's Final Fight
Speeches and Writings, 1922–23
V.I. Lenin

In the early 1920s Lenin waged his last political battle in the Communist Party leadership in the USSR to maintain the course that had enabled workers and peasants to overthrow the tsarist empire, carry out the first socialist revolution, and begin building a world communist movement. The issues posed in this fight—from the leadership's class composition, to the worker-peasant alliance and battle against national oppression—remain central to world politics today. $21. Also in Spanish.

Capitalism's World Disorder
Working-Class Politics at the Millennium
Jack Barnes

The social devastation and financial panic, coarsening of politics, cop brutality, and acts of imperialist aggression accelerating around us—all are the product not of something gone wrong with capitalism but of its lawful workings. Yet the future can be changed by the united struggle of workers and farmers conscious of their capacity to wage revolutionary struggle for state power and transform the world. $24. Also in Spanish and French.

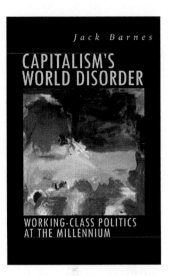

Jack Barnes

CAPITALISM'S WORLD DISORDER

WORKING-CLASS POLITICS AT THE MILLENNIUM

Imperialism's March toward Fascism and War
Jack Barnes

"There will be new Hitlers, new Mussolinis. That is inevitable. What is not inevitable is that they will triumph. The working-class vanguard will organize our class to fight back against the devastating toll we are made to pay for the capitalist crisis. The future of humanity will be decided in the contest between these contending class forces." In *New International* no. 10. $16. Also in Spanish, French, Icelandic, and Swedish.

Europe and America
Two Speeches on Imperialism
Leon Trotsky

Writing in the mid-1920s, Bolshevik leader Leon Trotsky explains the emergence of the United States as imperialism's dominant economic and financial power following World War I. He describes the sharpening conflicts between Washington and its European rivals and highlights the revolutionary openings for the working class that would be played out in the decade to come. Now with an index. $6

To Speak the Truth
Why Washington's 'Cold War' against Cuba Doesn't End
Fidel Castro, Ernesto Che Guevara

In historic speeches before the United Nations and UN bodies, Guevara and Castro address the peoples of the world, explaining why the U.S. government so fears the example set by the socialist revolution in Cuba and why Washington's effort to destroy it will fail. $17

Is Socialist Revolution in the U.S. Possible?
MARY-ALICE WATERS

Not only is socialist revolution in the U.S. possible, says Waters. Revolutionary struggles by working people are *inevitable*. As a fighting vanguard of the working class emerges in the U.S., the outlines of coming battles—whose outcome is *not* inevitable—can already be seen. The future depends on us. The sharp capitalist contraction of production and jobs that opened in late 2008, says Waters in the exanded edition, drives home this revolutionary perspective. $7. Also in Spanish and French.

Cuba and the Coming American Revolution
JACK BARNES

The Cuban Revolution of 1959 had a worldwide political impact, including on workers and youth in the imperialist heartland. As the proletarian-based struggle for Black rights was advancing in the U.S., the social transformation fought for and won by Cuban toilers set an example that socialist revolution is not only necessary—it can be made and defended. This second edition, with a new foreword by Mary-Alice Waters, should be read alongside *Is Socialist Revolution in the U.S. Possible?* $10. Also in Spanish and French.

Revolutionary Continuity
Marxist Leadership in the U.S.
FARRELL DOBBS

How successive generations of fighters joined in the struggles that shaped the U.S. labor movement, seeking to build a class-conscious revolutionary leadership capable of advancing the interests of workers and small farmers and linking up with fellow toilers worldwide. 2 vols. *The Early Years: 1848–1917,* $20; *Birth of the Communist Movement: 1918–1922,* $19

The Changing Face of U.S. Politics
Working-Class Politics and the Trade Unions
JACK BARNES

Building the kind of party working people need to prepare for coming class battles through which they will revolutionize themselves, their unions, and all society. A handbook for those seeking the road toward effective action to overturn the exploitative system of capitalism and join in reconstructing the world on new, socialist foundations. $24. Also in Spanish, French and Swedish.

Fighting Racism in World War II
C.L.R. JAMES, GEORGE BREITMAN, EDGAR KEEMER, AND OTHERS

A week-by-week account from 1939 to 1945 of efforts to advance the Black rights struggle in face of patriotic appeals to postpone resistance to lynch-mob terror and racist discrimination until after U.S. "victory" in World War II. These struggles—of a piece with rising anti-imperialist battles in Africa, Asia, and the Americas—helped lay the basis for the mass civil rights movement in the postwar decades. $22

Teamster Rebellion
FARRELL DOBBS

The 1934 strikes that built the industrial union movement in Minneapolis and helped pave the way for the CIO, recounted by a central leader of that battle. The first in a four-volume series on the class-struggle leadership of the strikes and organizing drives that transformed the Teamsters union in much of the Midwest into a fighting social movement and pointed the road toward independent labor political action. $19. Also in Spanish.

Socialism on Trial
JAMES P. CANNON

The basic ideas of socialism, explained in testimony during the 1941 trial of leaders of the Minneapolis Teamsters union and the Socialist Workers Party framed up and imprisoned under the notorious Smith "Gag" Act during World War II. $16. Also in Spanish.

Revolution in the United States

New International

A MAGAZINE OF MARXIST POLITICS AND THEORY

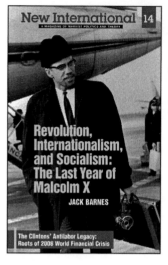

NEW INTERNATIONAL NO. 14

REVOLUTION, INTERNATIONALISM, AND SOCIALISM: THE LAST YEAR OF MALCOLM X

Jack Barnes

"To understand Malcolm's last year is to see how, in the imperialist epoch, revolutionary leadership of the highest political capacity, courage, and integrity converges with communism. That truth has even greater weight today as billions around the world, in city and countryside, from China to Brazil, are being hurled into the modern class struggle by the violent expansion of world capitalism."—Jack Barnes

Issue #14 also includes "The Clintons' Antilabor Legacy: Roots of the 2008 World Financial Crisis" *and* "Setting the Record Straight on Fascism and World War II." $14

NEW INTERNATIONAL NO. 8

CHE GUEVARA, CUBA, AND THE ROAD TO SOCIALISM

Articles by Ernesto Che Guevara, Carlos Rafael Rodríguez, Carlos Tablada, Mary-Alice Waters, Steve Clark, Jack Barnes

Exchanges from the opening years of the Cuban Revolution and today on the political perspectives defended by Guevara as he helped lead working people to advance the transformation of economic and social relations in Cuba. $10

PATHFINDER AROUND THE WORLD

Visit our website for a complete list of titles and to place orders

www.pathfinderpress.com

PATHFINDER DISTRIBUTORS

UNITED STATES
(and Caribbean, Latin America, and East Asia)

Pathfinder Books, 306 W. 37th St., 10th Floor,
New York, NY 10018

CANADA

Pathfinder Books, 7105 St. Hubert, Suite 106F,
Montreal, QC H2S 2N1

UNITED KINGDOM
(and Europe, Africa, Middle East, and South Asia)

Pathfinder Books, First Floor, 120 Bethnal Green Road
(entrance in Brick Lane), London E2 6DG

SWEDEN

Pathfinder böcker, Bildhuggarvägen 17, S-121 44 Johanneshov

AUSTRALIA
(and Southeast Asia and the Pacific)

Pathfinder, Level 1, 3/281-287 Beamish St., Campsie, NSW 2194
Postal address: P.O. Box 164, Campsie, NSW 2194

NEW ZEALAND

Pathfinder, 7 Mason Ave. (upstairs), Otahuhu, Auckland
Postal address: P.O. Box 3025, Auckland 1140

PATHFINDER READERS CLUB • CLUB DE LECTORES

NAME
NOMBRE ....
EXPIRATION DATE • FECHA QUE VENCE: ___/___/___
Valid at Pathfinder book centers and online
Válido en centros de libros Pathfinder y en línea
www.pathfinderpress.com

Join the Pathfinder Readers Club
to get 15% discounts on all Pathfinder titles
and bigger discounts on special offers.
Sign up at www.pathfinderpress.com
or through the distributors above.